THE FIFTH
AGREEMENT

A PRACTICAL GUIDE TO SELF-MASTERY

A Toltec
Wisdom Book

THE FIFTH
AGREEMENT

DON MIGUEL RUIZ
DON JOSE RUIZ
WITH JANET MILLS

AMBER-ALLEN PUBLISHING
SAN RAFAEL, CALIFORNIA

Published by Amber-Allen Publishing, Inc.
P. O. Box 6657
San Rafael, California 94903

Cover Illustration: Nicholas Wilton
Cover Design: Janet Mills
Typography: Rick Gordon

Library of Congress Cataloging-in-Publication Data

Ruiz, Miguel, 1952– The fifth agreement : a practical guide to self-mastery/
Miguel Angel Ruiz and Jose Luis Ruiz ; with Janet Mills. p. cm.
"A Toltec Wisdom book." ISBN 978-1-878424-61-7 (alk. paper)
1. Conduct of life. 2. Belief and doubt. 3. Toltec philosophy -- Miscellanea.
4. Ruiz, Miguel, 1952- Four agreements. I. Ruiz, Jose Luis, 1978-
II. Mills, Janet, 1953- III. Title.
BJ1595.R73 2010   299.7'92 — dc22   2009043960

Distributed by Hay House, Inc.

12 11 10 9 8 7 6

To every human who lives on this beautiful planet,
and to the generations to come.

CONTENTS

CONTENTS

PART II

Acknowledgments

THE AUTHORS WISH TO EXPRESS THEIR HEARTFELT gratitude to the following people: Janet Mills, the mother of this book; Judy Segal, for all her love and support; Ray Chambers, for lighting the way; Oprah Winfrey and Ellen DeGeneres, for sharing the message of *The Four Agreements* with so many people; Ed Rosenberg and Major General Riemer, for their recognition of *The Four Agreements* on the United States Air Force challenge coin; Gail Mills, Karen Kreiger, and Nancy Carleton, for generously contributing their time and talent to the realization of this book; and Joyce Mills, Maiya Champa,

ACKNOWLEDGMENTS

Dave McCullough, Theresa Nelson, and Shkiba Samimi-Amri for their dedication and ongoing support of the teachings of the Toltec.

The Toltec

THOUSANDS OF YEARS AGO, THE TOLTEC WERE known throughout southern Mexico as "women and men of knowledge." Anthropologists have spoken of the Toltec as a nation or a race, but, in fact, the Toltec were scientists and artists who formed a society to explore and conserve the spiritual knowledge and practices of the ancient ones. They came together as masters (*naguals*) and students at Teotihuacan, the ancient city of pyramids outside Mexico City known as the place where "Man Becomes God." Over the millennia, the *naguals* were forced to conceal the ancestral wisdom and maintain its existence in obscurity.

European conquest, coupled with rampant misuse of personal power by a few of the apprentices, made it necessary to shield the knowledge from those who were not prepared to use it wisely or who might intentionally misuse it for personal gain.

Fortunately, the esoteric Toltec knowledge was embodied and passed on through generations by different lineages of *naguals.* Though it remained veiled in secrecy for hundreds of years, ancient prophecies foretold the coming of an age when it would be necessary to return the wisdom to the people. Now, don Miguel Ruiz and don Jose Ruiz (*naguals* from the Eagle Knight lineage) have been guided to share with us the powerful teachings of the Toltec.

Toltec wisdom arises from the same essential unity of truth as all the sacred esoteric traditions found around the world. Though it is not a religion, it honors all the spiritual masters who have taught on the earth. While it does embrace spirit, it is most accurately described as a way of life, distinguished by the ready accessibility of happiness and love.

Introduction
by don Miguel Ruiz

THE FOUR AGREEMENTS WAS PUBLISHED MANY YEARS ago. If you have read the book, you already know what these agreements can do. They have the ability to transform your life by breaking thousands of limiting agreements you have made with yourself, with other people, with *life* itself.

The first time you read *The Four Agreements*, it begins to work its magic. It goes much deeper than the words you are reading. You feel that you already know every word in the book. You feel it, but perhaps you never put it into words. When you read the book the first time, it challenges what you believe, and takes you to the limit of your comprehension. You break many limiting agreements, and overcome many challenges, but then you see new challenges. When you read the book a second time, it feels as if you're reading a completely different book because the limits of your comprehension have already grown. Once again, it takes you into a deeper awareness of yourself, and you reach the limit that you can reach in that moment. And when you read the book a third time, it's just as if you're reading another book.

Just like magic, because they *are* magic, the Four Agreements slowly help you to recover your authentic self. With practice, these four simple agreements take you to what you *really* are, not what you pretend to be, and this is exactly where you want to be: what you really are.

The principles in *The Four Agreements* speak to the heart of all human beings, from the young to the old. They speak to people of different cultures all around the world — people who speak different languages, people whose religious and philosophical beliefs are vastly different. They have been taught at different kinds of schools, from elementary schools to secondary schools to universities. The principles in *The Four Agreements* reach everyone because they are pure common sense.

Now it's time to give another gift: *The Fifth Agreement.* The fifth agreement wasn't included in my first book because the first four agreements were enough of a challenge at that time. The fifth agreement is made with words, of course, but its meaning and intent is beyond the words. The fifth agreement is ultimately about seeing your whole reality with the eyes of truth, *without* words. The result of practicing the fifth agreement is the complete acceptance of yourself just the way you are, and the complete acceptance of everybody else just the way they are. The reward is your eternal happiness.

Many years ago, I began teaching some of the concepts in this book to my apprentices, but then I stopped because nobody seemed to understand what I was trying to say. Though I had shared the fifth agreement with my apprentices, I discovered that nobody was ready to learn the teachings that underlie this agreement. Years later, my son, don Jose, started to share the same teachings with a group of students, and he succeeded where I had failed. Maybe the reason don Jose was successful was because he had complete faith in sharing the message. His very presence spoke the truth and challenged the beliefs of the people who attended his classes. He made a huge difference in their lives.

Don Jose Ruiz has been my apprentice since he was a child, since he learned to speak. In this book, I am honored to introduce my son, and to present the essence of the teachings we delivered together over a period of seven years.

To keep the message as personal as possible, and in keeping with the first-person voice of prior books in the Toltec Wisdom series, we have opted to present *The Fifth Agreement* in the same first-person style of writing. In this book, we speak to the reader with one voice, and with one heart.

PART I

❧

THE POWER OF SYMBOLS

1

IN THE BEGINNING

It's All in the Program

FROM THE MOMENT YOU ARE BORN, YOU DELIVER a message to the world. What is the message? The message is *you*, that child. It's the presence of an *angel*, a messenger from the infinite in a human body. The infinite, a total power, creates a program just for you, and everything you need to be what you are is in the program. You are born, you grow up, you mate, you grow old, and in the end you return to the infinite. Every cell in your body is a universe of its own. It's intelligent, it's complete, and it's programmed to be whatever it is.

You are programmed to be *you*, whatever you are, and it makes no difference to the program what your mind *thinks* you are. The program is not in the thinking mind. It's in the body, in what we call the *DNA*, and in the beginning, you instinctively follow its wisdom. As a very young child, you know what you like, what you don't like, when you like it, when you don't. You follow what you like, and you try to avoid what you don't like. You follow your instincts, and those instincts guide you to be happy, to enjoy life, to play, to love, to fulfill your needs. Then what happens?

Your body begins to develop, your mind begins to mature, and you begin to use symbols to deliver your message. Just as the birds understand the birds, and the cats understand the cats, the humans understand the humans through a symbology. If you were born on an island and then lived all alone, it might take you ten years, but you would give a name to everything that you see, and you would use that language to communicate a message, even if it was only to yourself. Why would you do this? Well, it's easy to understand, and it's not because humans are so intelligent. It's because we are programmed to create a language, to invent an entire symbology for ourselves.

As you know, all around the world humans speak and write in thousands of different languages. Humans have invented all kinds of symbols to communicate not only with other humans but more importantly with ourselves. The symbols can be sounds that we speak, motions that we make, or handwriting and signs that are graphic in nature. There are symbols for objects, ideas, music, and mathematics, but the introduction of sounds is the very first step, which means we learn to use symbols to speak.

The humans who come before us already have names for everything that exists, and they teach us the meaning of sounds. They call this a *table*; they call that a *chair*. They also have names for things that only exist in our imagination, like mermaids and unicorns. Every word that we learn is a symbol for something real or imagined, and there are thousands of words to learn. If we observe children who are one to four years old, we can see the effort they make trying to learn an entire symbology. It's a big effort that we usually don't remember because our mind is not yet mature, but with repetition and practice we finally learn to speak.

Once we learn to speak, the humans who take care of us teach us what they know, which means they program us with knowledge. The humans we live with have lots of knowledge, including all the social, religious, and moral rules of their culture. They hook our attention, pass on the information, and teach us to be like them. We learn how to be a man or a woman according to the society in which we are born. We learn how to behave the "right" way in our society, which means how to be a "good" human.

In truth, we are domesticated the same way that a dog, a cat, or any animal is domesticated: through a system of punishment and reward. We are told that we're a *good boy* or a *good girl* when we do what the grown-ups want us to do; we're a *bad boy* or a *bad girl* when we don't do what they want us to do. Sometimes we are punished without being bad, and sometimes we are rewarded without being good. Out of fear of being punished and fear of not getting a reward, we start trying to please other people. We try to be good, because bad people don't receive rewards; they are punished.

In human domestication, all the rules and values of our family and society are imposed on us. We don't have the opportunity to choose our beliefs; we are told what to believe, and what not to believe. The people we live with tell us their opinions: what is good and what is bad, what is right and what is wrong, what is beautiful and what is ugly. Just like a computer, all that information is downloaded into our head. We are innocent; we *believe* what our parents or other grown-ups tell us; we *agree*, and the information is stored in our memory. Everything we learn goes into our mind by agreement, and it stays in our mind by agreement, but first it goes through the attention.

The attention is very important in humans because it's the part of the mind that makes it possible for us to concentrate on a single object or thought out of a whole range of possibilities. Through the attention, information from the outside is conveyed to the inside and vice versa. The attention is the channel we use to send and receive messages from human to human. It's like a bridge from one mind to another mind; we open the bridge with sounds, signs, symbols, touch — with any event that hooks the attention. This is how we teach, and this is how we learn. We cannot teach anything if we don't have someone's attention; we cannot learn anything if we don't pay attention.

Using the attention, the grown-ups teach us how to create an entire reality in our mind with the use of symbols. After they teach us a symbology by sound, the grown-ups drill us with our ABCs, and we learn the same language, but graphically. Our imagination begins to develop, our curiosity grows stronger, and we start to ask questions. We ask and ask, and we keep asking questions; we gather information from everywhere. And we know that we've finally mastered a language when we are able to use the symbols to talk to ourselves in our head. This is when we learn to *think*. Before that, we don't think; we mimic sounds and use symbols to communicate, but life is simple before we attach any meaning or emotion to the symbols.

Once we give meaning to the symbols, we begin to use them to try to make sense of everything that happens in our lives. We use the symbols to think about things that are real, and to think about things that aren't real, but that we start to imagine are real, like beautiful and ugly, skinny and fat, smart and stupid. And if you notice, we can only think in a language that we master. For many years, I spoke only Spanish, and it took a long time for me to master enough symbols in English to think in English. To master a language is not easy, but at a certain point, we find ourselves *thinking* with the symbols we learn.

By the time we go to school, when we are five or six years old, we understand the meaning of abstract concepts like right and wrong, winner and loser, perfect and imperfect. In school, we continue to learn how to read and write the symbols we already know, and the written language makes it possible for us to accumulate more knowledge. We continue to give meaning to more and more symbols, and thinking becomes not only effortless but automatic.

Now the symbols that we learned are hooking our attention all by themselves. It's what we know that's talking to us, and we are listening to what our knowledge says. I call it *the voice of knowledge* because knowledge is talking in our head. Many times we hear the voice with different tonalities; we hear the voice of our mother, our father, our brothers and sisters, and the voice never stops talking. The voice isn't real; it's our creation. But we *believe* that it's real because we give it life through the power of our faith, which means we believe *without a doubt* what that voice is telling us. This is when the opinions of the humans around us start taking over our mind.

Everybody has an opinion of us, and they tell us what we are. As very young children, we don't know what we are. The only way we can see ourselves is through a mirror, and other people act as that mirror. Our mother tells us what we are, and we believe her. It's completely different from what our father tells us, or what our brothers and sisters tell us, but we agree with them, too. People tell us how we look, and it's especially true when we are little children. "Look, you have the eyes of your mother, the nose of your grandfather." We listen to all the opinions of our family, our teachers, and the big children at school. We see our image in those mirrors, we agree that this is what we are, and as soon as we agree, that opinion becomes a part of our belief system. Little by little, all these opinions modify our behavior, and in our mind we form an image of ourselves according to what other people say we are: "I'm beautiful; I'm not so beautiful. I'm smart; I'm not so smart. I'm a winner; I'm a loser. I'm good at this; I'm bad at that."

At a certain point, all the opinions of our parents and teachers, religion and society, make us believe that we need to be a certain way in order to be accepted.

They tell us the way we *should* be, the way we *should* look, the way we *should* behave. We need to be *this* way; we shouldn't be *that* way — and because it's not okay for us to be what we are, we start pretending to be what we are not. The fear of being rejected becomes the fear of not being good enough, and we start searching for something that we call *perfection*. In our search, we form an image of perfection, the way we wish to be, but we know that we are not, and we begin to judge ourselves for that. We don't like ourselves, and we tell ourselves, "Look how silly you look, how ugly you are. Look how fat, how short, how weak, how stupid you are." This is when the drama begins, because now the symbols are going against us. We don't even notice that we've learned to use the symbols to reject ourselves.

Before domestication, we don't care what we are or what we look like. Our tendency is to explore, to express our creativity, to seek pleasure and avoid pain. As little children, we are wild and free; we run around naked without self-consciousness or self-judgment.

We speak the truth because we live in truth. Our attention is in the moment; we are not afraid of the future or ashamed of the past. After domestication, we try to be good enough for everybody else, but we are no longer good enough for ourselves, because we can never live up to our image of perfection.

All of our normal human tendencies are lost in the process of domestication, and we begin to search for what we have lost. We start searching for freedom because we are no longer free to be what we really are; we start searching for happiness because we are no longer happy; we start searching for beauty because we no longer believe that we are beautiful.

We continue to grow, and in our adolescence, our body is programmed to introduce a substance we call *hormones*. Our physical body is no longer a child's, and we don't fit in with the way of life we lived before. We don't want to hear our parents tell us what to do and what not to do. We want our freedom; we want to be ourselves, but we are also afraid to be by ourselves. People tell us, "You're not a child anymore," but we're not an adult either, and it's a difficult time for most humans. By the time we are teenagers, we don't need anyone to domesticate us; we have learned to judge ourselves, punish ourselves, and reward ourselves according to the same belief system we were given, and using the same system of punishment and reward. The domestication may be easier for people in some places in the world, and harder for people in other places, but in general none of us has a chance of escaping the domestication. None of us.

Finally, the body matures and everything changes again. We start searching once again, but now, more and more, what we are searching for is our *self*. We are searching for love because we have learned to believe that love is somewhere outside of us; we are searching for justice because there is no justice in the belief system we were taught; we are searching for truth because we only believe in the knowledge we have stored in our mind. And of course, we're still searching for perfection because now we agree with the rest of the humans that "nobody's perfect."

2

SYMBOLS AND AGREEMENTS

The Art of Humans

DURING ALL THE YEARS THAT WE GROW UP, WE MAKE countless agreements with ourselves, with society, with everybody around us. But the most important agreements are the ones we make with ourselves by understanding the symbols we learned. The symbols are telling us what we believe about ourselves; they're telling us what we are and what we are not, what is possible and what is not possible. The voice of knowledge is telling us everything that we know, but who tells us if what we know is the truth?

When we go to grammar school, high school, and college, we acquire a lot of knowledge, but what do we really know? Do we master the truth? No, we master a language, a symbology, and that symbology is only the truth because we *agree*, not because it's *really* the truth. Wherever we are born, whatever language we learn to speak, we find that almost everything we know is really about agreements, beginning with the symbols that we learn.

If we are born in England, we learn English symbols. If we are born in China, we learn Chinese symbols. But whether we learn English, Chinese, Spanish, German, Russian, or any other language, the symbols only have value because we assign them a value and agree on their meaning. If we don't agree, the symbols are meaningless. The word *tree*, for example, is meaningful for people who speak English, but "tree" doesn't mean anything unless we *believe* that it means something, unless we *agree*. What it means for you, it means for me, and that's why we understand one another. What I'm saying right now you understand because we agree with the meaning of every word that was programmed in our mind. But this doesn't mean that we completely agree. Each of us gives a meaning to every word, and it's not exactly the same for everyone.

If we focus our attention on the way any word is created, we find that whatever meaning we give to a word is there for no real reason. We put words together from nowhere; we make them up. Humans invent every sound, every letter, every graphic symbol. We hear a sound like "A" and we say, "This is the symbol for that sound." We draw a symbol to represent the sound, we put the symbol and the sound together, and we give it a meaning. Then every word in our mind has a meaning, but not because it's real, not because it's truth. It's just an agreement with ourselves, and with everybody else who learns the same symbology.

If we travel to a country where people speak a different language, we suddenly realize the importance and power of agreement. Un árbol es sólo un árbol, el sol es sólo el sol, la tierra es sólo la tierra si estamos de acuerdo. Ένα δέντρο είναι μονάχα ένα δέντρο, ο ήλιος είναι μονάχα ο ήλιος, η γη είναι μονάχα η γη, αν συμφωνούμε. Ein Baum ist nur ein Baum, die Sonne ist nur die Sonne, die Erde ist nur die Erde wenn wir uns darauf verständigt haben. 樹只是樹，太陽只是太陽，土地就是土地，只要我們也這樣想. A *tree* is only a *tree*, the *sun* is only the *sun*, the *earth* is only the *earth* if we agree. These symbols have no meaning in France, Russia, Turkey, Sweden, or in any other place where the agreements are different.

If we learn to speak English and we go to China, we hear people talking, but we don't understand a word they are saying. Nothing makes sense to us because it's not the symbology that we learned. Many things are foreign to us; it's like being in another world. If we visit their places of worship, we find that their beliefs are completely different, their rituals are completely different, their mythologies have nothing to do with what we learned. One way to understand their culture is to learn the symbols they use, which means their language, but if we learn a new way of being, a new religion or philosophy, this may create a conflict with what we learned before. New beliefs clash with old beliefs, and the doubt comes right away: "What is right and what is wrong? Is it true what I learned before? Is it true what I'm learning right now? What is the truth?"

The truth is that all of our knowledge, 100 percent of it, is nothing more than symbolism or words that we invent for the need to understand and express what we perceive. Every word in our mind and on this page is just a symbol, but every word has the power of our faith because we *believe* in its meaning without a doubt. Humans construct an entire belief system made up of symbols; we build an entire edifice of knowledge. Then we use everything we know, which is nothing but symbology, to justify what we believe, to try to explain first to ourselves, then to everybody around us, the way we perceive ourselves, the way we perceive the entire universe.

If we are aware of this, then it's easy to understand that all of the different mythologies, religions, and philosophies around the world, all of the different beliefs and ways of thinking, are nothing but agreements with ourselves and with other humans. They're our creation, but are they true? Everything that exists is true: the earth is true, the stars are true, the entire universe has always been true. But the symbols that we use to construct what we know are only true because we say so.

᠁

There's a beautiful story in the Bible that illustrates the relationship between God and humans. In this story, Adam and God are walking together around the world, and God asks Adam what he wants to name everything. One by one, Adam gives a name to everything he perceives. "Let's call this a *tree*. Let's call this a *bird*. Let's call this a *flower*. . . ." And God agrees with Adam. The story is about the creation of symbols, the creation of an entire language, and it works by agreement.

It's like two sides of the same coin: We can say that one side is pure perception, what Adam perceives; the other side is the meaning that Adam gives to whatever he perceives. There's the object of perception, which is the truth, and there's our interpretation of the truth, which is just a point of view. The truth is objective, and we call it *science*. Our interpretation of the truth is subjective, and we call it *art*. Science and art; the truth, and our interpretation of the truth. The real truth is life's creation, and it's the absolute truth because it's truth for everyone. Our interpretation of the truth is our creation, and it's a relative truth because it's only truth by agreement. With this awareness, we can begin to understand the human mind.

All humans are programmed to perceive the truth, and we don't need a language to do this. But in order to *express* the truth, we need to use a language, and that expression is our art. It's no longer the truth because words are symbols, and symbols can only represent or "symbolize" the truth. For example, we can see a tree even if we don't know the symbol "tree." Without the symbol, we just see an object. The object is real, it is truth, and we perceive it. Once we call it a *tree*, we are using art to express a point of view. By using more symbols, we can describe the tree — every leaf, every color. We can say it's a big tree, a small tree, a beautiful tree, an ugly tree, but is it the truth? No, the tree is still the same tree.

Our interpretation of the tree will depend on our emotional reaction to the tree, and our emotional reaction will depend on the symbols that we use to re-create the tree in our mind. As you can see, our interpretation of the tree is not exactly the truth. But our interpretation is a *reflection* of the truth, and that reflection is what we call the *human mind*. The human mind is nothing but a virtual reality. It isn't real. What's real is truth. What's truth is truth for everyone. But the virtual reality is our personal creation; it's our art, and it's only "truth" for each one of us.

All humans are artists, *all* of us. Every symbol, every word, is a little piece of art. From my point of view, and thanks to our programming, our greatest masterpiece of art is the use of a language to create an entire virtual reality within our mind. The virtual reality we create could be a clear reflection of the truth, or it could be completely distorted. Either way, it's art. Our creation could be our personal heaven, or it could be our personal hell. It doesn't matter; it's art. But what we can do with the awareness of what is truth and what is virtual is endless. The truth leads to self-mastery, to a life that's very easy; our distortion of the truth often leads to needless conflict and human suffering. Awareness makes all the difference.

Humans are born with awareness; we are born to perceive the truth, but we accumulate knowledge, and we learn to deny what we perceive. We practice not being aware, and we master not being aware. The word is pure magic, and we learn to use our magic against ourselves, against creation, against our own kind. To be aware means to open our eyes to see the truth. When we see the truth, we see everything just as it is, not the way we believe it is, not the way we wish it to be. Awareness opens the door to millions of possibilities, and if we know that we are the artist of our own life, we can make a choice from all those possibilities.

What I'm sharing with you comes from my personal training, which I call *Toltec Wisdom. Toltec* is a Náhuatl word meaning *artist*. From my point of view, to be a *Toltec* has nothing to do with any philosophy or place in the world. To be a Toltec is just to be an artist. A Toltec is an artist of the spirit, and as artists we like beauty; we don't like what is not beauty. If we become better artists, our virtual reality becomes a better reflection of the truth, and we can create a masterpiece of heaven with our art.

Thousands of years ago, the Toltec created three masteries of the artist: *the mastery of awareness, the mastery of transformation,* and *the mastery of love, intent,* or *faith.* The separation is just for our understanding, because the three masteries become only one. The truth is only one, and the truth is what we are talking about. These three masteries guide us out of suffering and return us to our true nature, which is happiness, freedom, and love.

The Toltec understood that we are going to create a virtual reality with or without awareness. If it's with awareness, we're going to enjoy our creation. And whether we facilitate the transformation or resist it, our virtual reality is always transforming. If we practice the art of transformation, soon we're facilitating the transformation, and instead of using our magic against ourselves, we are using our magic for the expression of our happiness and our love. When we master love, intent, or faith, we master the dream of our life, and when all three masteries are accomplished, we reclaim our divinity and become one with God. This is the goal of the Toltec.

The Toltec didn't have the technology that we have at the present time; they didn't know about the virtual reality of computers, but they knew how to master the virtual reality of the human mind. The mastery of the human mind requires complete control of the attention — the way we interpret and react to information we perceive from inside of us and outside of us. The Toltec understood that each one of us is just like God, but instead of creating, we re-create. And what do we re-create? What we perceive. That is what becomes the human mind.

If we can understand what the human mind is, and what the human mind does, we can begin to separate reality from virtual reality, or pure perception, which is truth, from symbology, which is art. Self-mastery is all about awareness, and it begins with self-awareness. First to be aware of what is real, and then to be aware of what is virtual, which means what we believe about what is real. With this awareness, we know that we can change what is virtual by changing what we believe. What is real we cannot change, and it doesn't matter what we believe.

3

The Story of You

The First Agreement:
Be Impeccable with Your Word

FOR THOUSANDS OF YEARS HUMANS HAVE TRIED to understand the universe, nature, and mainly *human* nature. It's amazing to observe humans in action all around the world, in all the different places and cultures that exist on this beautiful planet Earth. Humans make a lot of effort to understand, but in doing so we also make a lot of assumptions. As artists, we distort the truth and create the most amazing theories; we create entire philosophies and the most amazing religions; we create stories and superstitions about everything, including ourselves. And this is exactly the main point: *We create them.*

Humans are born with the power of creation, and we are constantly creating stories with the words that we learned. Every one of us uses the word to form our opinions, to express our point of view. Countless events are happening all around us, and using the attention, we have the capacity to put all these events together in a story. We create the story of our own life, the story of our family, the story of our community, the story of our country, the story of humanity, the story of the entire world. Every one of us has a story that we share, a message that we deliver to ourselves, and to everyone and everything around us.

You were programmed to deliver a message, and the creation of that message is your greatest art.

What is the message? Your *life*. With that message, you create mainly the story of you, and then a story about everything you perceive. You create an entire virtual reality in your mind, and you live in that reality. When you think, you're thinking in your language; you're repeating in your mind all those symbols that mean something to you. You're giving yourself a message, and that message is the truth for you because you believe that it's the truth.

The story of you is everything that you know about you, and when I say this, I'm talking to you, knowledge, what you believe you are, not to *you*, the human, what you *really* are. As you can see, I make a distinction between you and *you* because one of you is real, and one of you is not real. *You*, the physical human, are real; *you* are the truth. You, knowledge — you're not real; you're virtual. You only exist because of the agreements you made with yourself and with the other humans around you. You, knowledge, come from the symbols you hear in your head, from all the opinions of the people you love, the people you don't love, the people you know, and mostly the people you'll never know.

Who is talking in your head? You make the assumption that it's you. But if you are the one who is talking, then who is listening? You, knowledge, are the one who is talking in your head, telling you what you are. *You*, the human, are listening, but *you*, the human, existed long before you had knowledge. You existed long before you understood all those symbols, before you learned to speak, and just like any child before he or she learns to speak, you were completely authentic. You didn't pretend to be what you are not. Without even knowing it, you trusted yourself completely; you loved yourself completely. Before you learned knowledge, you were totally free to be what you really are because all those opinions and stories from other humans were not in your head already.

Your mind is full of knowledge, but how are you *using* that knowledge? How are you using the word when it comes to describing yourself? When you look at yourself in a mirror, do you like what you see, or do you judge your body and use all those symbols to tell yourself lies? Is it *really* true that you are too short or too tall, too heavy or too thin? Is it *really* true that you are not beautiful? Is it *really* true that you're not perfect just the way you are?

Can you see all the judgments that you have about yourself? Every judgment is just an opinion — it's just a point of view — and that point of view wasn't there when you were born. Everything you think about yourself, everything you believe about yourself, is because you learned it. You learned the opinions from Mom, Dad, siblings, and society. They sent all those images of how a body should look; they expressed all those opinions about the way you are, the way you are not, the way you *should* be. They delivered a message, and you agreed with that message. And now you think so many things about what you are, but are they the truth?

You see, the problem is not really knowledge; the problem is believing in a *distortion* of knowledge

— and that is what we call a *lie*. What is the truth, and what is the lie? What is real, and what is virtual? Can you see the difference, or do you believe that voice in your head every time it speaks and distorts the truth while assuring you that what you believe is the way things really are? Is it *really* true that you're not a good human, and that you'll never be good enough? Is it *really* true that you don't deserve to be happy? Is it *really* true that you're not worthy of love?

Remember when a tree was no longer just a tree? Once you learn a language, you interpret a tree and judge a tree according to everything that you know. That's when a tree becomes the beautiful tree, the ugly tree, the scary tree, the wonderful tree. Well, you do the same thing with yourself. You interpret yourself and judge yourself according to everything that you know. That's when you become the good human, the bad human, the guilty one, the crazy one, the powerful one, the weak one, the beautiful one, the ugly one. You are what you believe you are. Then the first question is: "What do you believe you are?"

If you use your awareness, you will see everything you believe, and this is how you live your life. Your life is totally dominated by the system of beliefs that you learned. Whatever you believe is creating the story that you're experiencing; whatever you believe is creating the emotions that you're experiencing. And you may really want to believe that you *are* what you believe, but that image is completely false. It's not *you*.

The real you is unique and it's beyond everything that you know, because the real you is the truth. You, the human, are the truth. Your physical presence is real. What you believe about yourself is not real, and it's not important unless you want to create a better story for yourself. Truth or fiction; either way, the story that you're creating is a work of art. It's a wonderful story, a beautiful story, but it's just a story, and it's as close to the truth as you can get by using symbols.

As an artist, there is no right or wrong way to create your art; there's just beauty or there's not beauty; there's happiness or there's not happiness. If you believe yourself to be an artist, then everything becomes possible again. Words are your paintbrush, and your life is the canvas. You can paint whatever you want to paint; you can even copy another artist's work — but what you express with your paintbrush is the way you see yourself, the way you see the entire reality. What you paint is your life, and how it looks will depend on how you are using the word. When you realize this, it may dawn on you that the word is a powerful tool for creation. When you learn to use that tool with awareness, you can make history with the word. What history? Your life's history, of course. The story of *you*.

THE FIRST AGREEMENT:
BE IMPECCABLE WITH YOUR WORD

This brings us to the first and most important of the Four Agreements: *Be impeccable with your word.* The word is your power of creation, and that power can be used in more than one direction. One direction is impeccability, where the word creates a beautiful story — your personal heaven on earth. The other direction is misuse of the word, where the word destroys everything around you, and creates your personal hell.

The word, as a symbol, has the magic and power of creation because it can reproduce an image, an idea, a feeling, or an entire story in your imagination. Just hearing the word *horse* can reproduce an entire image in your mind. That's the power of a symbol. But it can even be more powerful than that. Just by saying two words, *The Godfather*, a whole movie can appear in your mind. This is your magic, your power of creation, and it begins with the word.

Perhaps you can understand why the Bible says, "In the beginning was the word, and the word was with God, and the word was God." According to many religions, in the beginning, nothing existed, and the very first thing that God created was the messenger, the angel who delivers a message. You may understand the need for something that could transfer information from one place to another place. Of course, from nowhere to nowhere seems a little complicated, but it's very simple at the same time. In the very beginning, God created the word, and the *word* is a messenger. Then if God created the word to deliver a message, and if the word is a messenger, then that is what you are: a messenger, an angel.

The word exists because of a force that we call *life, intent,* or *God.* The word *is* the force; it *is* the intent, and that's why our intent manifests through the word no matter what language we speak. The word is so important in the creation of everything, because the messenger starts to deliver messages, and the entire creation appears out of nowhere.

Remember God and Adam talking and walking together? God creates reality, and we re-create reality with the word. The virtual reality that we create is a reflection of reality; it's our interpretation of reality by use of the word. Nothing can exist without the word, because the word is what we use to create everything that we know.

If you notice, I'm changing all the symbols on purpose, so you can see that the different expressions mean the exact same thing. The symbols can change, but the meaning is the same in all the different traditions around the world. If you listen to the intent *behind* the symbols, you will understand what I'm trying to say. Impeccability of the word is so important because the word is *you*, the messenger. The word is all about the message you deliver, not just to everyone and everything around you, but the message you deliver to yourself.

You're telling yourself a story, but is it the truth? If you're using the word to create a story with self-judgment and self-rejection, then you're using the word against yourself, and you're not being impeccable. When you're impeccable, you're not going to tell yourself, "I'm old. I'm ugly. I'm fat. I'm not good enough. I'm not strong enough. I'm never going to make it in life." You're not going to use your knowledge against yourself, which means your voice of knowledge is not going to use the word to judge you, find you guilty, and punish you. Your mind is so powerful that it perceives the story that you create. If you create self-judgment, you create inner conflict that's nothing but a nightmare.

Your happiness is up to you, and it depends on how you use the word. If you get angry and use the word to send emotional poison to someone else, it appears that you're using the word against that person, but you're really using the word against yourself. That action is going to create a like reaction, and that person is going to go against *you*. If you insult someone, that person may even harm you in response. If you use the word to create a conflict in which your body may be injured, of course it's against you.

Be impeccable with your word really means never use the power of the word against *yourself*. When you're impeccable with your word, you never betray yourself. You never use the word to gossip about yourself or to spread emotional poison by gossiping about other people. Gossiping is the main form of communication in human society, and we learn how to gossip by agreement. When we are children, we hear the adults around us gossiping about themselves, and giving their opinions about other people, including people they don't even know. But now you are aware that our opinions are not the truth; they're just a point of view.

Remember, you are the creator of your own life story. If you use the word impeccably, just imagine the story that you are going to create for yourself. You're going to use the word in the direction of truth and love for yourself. You're going to use the word to express the truth in every thought, in every action, in every word you use to describe yourself, to describe your own life story. And what will be the result? An extraordinarily beautiful life. In other words, you are going to be happy.

As you can see, impeccability of the word goes much deeper than it seems. The word is pure magic, and when you adopt the first agreement, magic just happens in your life. Your intentions and desires come easily because there is no resistance, there is no fear; there is only love. You are at peace, and you create a life of freedom and fulfillment in every way. Just this one agreement is enough to completely transform your life into your personal heaven. Always be aware of how you are using the word, and *be impeccable with your word.*

4

EVERY MIND IS A WORLD

The Second Agreement:
Don't Take Anything Personally

WHEN WE ARE BORN, THERE ARE NO SYMBOLS IN
our mind, but we have a brain and we have eyes, and
our brain is already capturing images that come
from light. We start perceiving light, we become
familiar with light, and the reaction of our brain to
light is an endless play of images in our imagination,

in our mind. We are *dreaming*. From the Toltec point of view, our whole life is a dream because the brain is programmed to dream twenty-four hours a day.

When the brain is awake, there is a material frame that makes us perceive things in a linear way; when the brain is asleep, there is no frame, and the dream has the tendency to change constantly. Even with the brain awake, we have the tendency to daydream, and the dream is constantly changing. The imagination is so powerful that it takes us to many places. We see things in our imagination that other people don't see; we hear things that other people don't hear, or maybe we don't, depending on the way we dream. Imagination gives movement to the images we see, but the images only exist in the mind, in the dream.

Light, images, imagination, dreaming. . . . You are dreaming right now, and this is something that you can easily verify. Perhaps you never noticed that your mind is always dreaming, but if you use your imagination for just a moment, you will understand what I'm trying to explain to you. Imagine that you are looking into a mirror. Inside the mirror is a whole world of objects, but you know that what you see is just a reflection of what is real. It looks like it's real, it looks like the truth, but it's not real and it's not the truth. If you try to touch the objects inside the mirror, you only touch the surface of the mirror.

What you see inside the mirror is just an *image* of reality, which means it's a *virtual* reality; it's a dream. And it's the same kind of dream that humans dream with the brain awake. Why? Because what you see inside the mirror is a copy of reality that you create with the capacity of your eyes and your brain. It's an *image* of the world that you construct within your mind, which means it's how your own mind perceives reality. What a dog sees in the mirror is how the dog's brain perceives reality. What an eagle sees in that same mirror is how the eagle's brain perceives reality, and it's different from your own.

Now imagine looking into your eyes instead of a mirror. Your eyes perceive light that's being reflected from millions of objects outside of your eyes. The sun sends light all around the world, and every object reflects light. Billions of rays of light come from everywhere, go inside your eyes, and project images of objects in your eyes. You think you are seeing all these objects, but the only thing you are *really* seeing is light that's being reflected.

Everything you perceive is a reflection of what is real, just like the reflections in a mirror, except for one important difference. Behind the mirror there is nothing, but behind your eyes is a brain that tries to make sense of everything. Your brain is interpreting everything you perceive according to the meaning you give to every symbol, according to the structure of your language, according to all of the knowledge that was programmed in your mind. Everything you perceive is being filtered through your entire belief system. And the result of interpreting everything you perceive by using everything you believe is your personal dream. This is how you create an entire virtual reality in your mind.

Perhaps you can see how easy it is for humans to distort what we perceive. Light reproduces a perfect image of what is real, but we distort the image by creating a story with all those symbols and opinions that we learned. We dream about it with our imagination, and by agreement we think that our dream is the absolute truth, when the real truth is that our dream is a relative truth, a *reflection* of the truth that is always going to be distorted by all the knowledge we have stored in our memory.

Many masters have said that every mind is a world, and it's true. The world we think we see outside of us is actually *inside* of us. It's just *images* in our imagination. It's a *dream*. We are dreaming constantly, and this has been known for centuries, not only in Mexico by the Toltec, but in Greece, in Rome, in India, in Egypt. People all over the world have said, "Life is a dream." The question is, are we aware of it?

When we aren't aware that our mind is always dreaming, it's easy to blame everyone and everything outside of us for all the distortions in our personal dream, for anything that makes us suffer in life. When we become aware that we are living in a dream that we artists are creating, we take a big step in our own evolution because now we can take responsibility for our creation. To realize that our mind is always dreaming gives us the key to changing our dream if we're not enjoying it.

Who is dreaming the story of your life? You are. If you don't like your life, if you don't like what you believe about yourself, you are the only one who can change it. It's your world; it's your dream. If you're enjoying your dream, that's wonderful; then continue to enjoy each and every moment. If your dream is a nightmare, if there's drama and suffering, and you're not enjoying your creation, then you can change it. As I'm sure you are aware, there are millions of books in this world written by millions of dreamers with different points of view. The story of you is as interesting as any of those books, and it's even more interesting because your story continues to change. The way you dream when you are ten years old is completely different from the way you dream when you are fifteen or when you are twenty, or thirty, or forty, or the way you dream now.

The story you're dreaming today is not the same story that you were dreaming yesterday, or even half an hour ago. Every time you talk about your story, it changes depending on who you're telling the story to, depending on your physical and emotional state at the time, depending on your beliefs at the time. Even if you try to tell the same story, your story is always changing. At a certain point, you find out that it's nothing but a story. It isn't reality; it's a virtual reality. It's nothing but a dream. And it's a shared dream because all humans are dreaming at the same time. The shared dream of humanity, *the dream of the planet*, was there before you were born, and this is how you learned to create your own art, the story of you.

The Second Agreement:
Don't Take Anything Personally

Let's use the power of our imagination to create a dream together, knowing that it's a dream. Imagine that you are in a gigantic mall where there are hundreds of movie theaters. You look around to see what's playing, and you notice a movie that has your name. Amazing! You go inside the theater, and it's empty except for one person. Very quietly, trying not to interrupt, you sit behind that person, who doesn't even notice you; all that person's attention is on the movie.

You look at the screen, and what a big surprise! You recognize every character in the movie — your mother, your father, your brothers and sisters, your beloved, your children, your friends. Then you see the main character of the movie, and it's you! You are the star of the movie and it's the story of you. And that person in front of you, well, it's also you, watching yourself act in the movie. Of course, the main character is just the way you believe you are, and so are all the secondary characters because you know the story of you. After a while, you feel a little overwhelmed by everything you just witnessed, and you decide to go to another theater.

In this theater there is also just one person watching a movie, and she doesn't even notice when you sit beside her. You start watching the movie, and you recognize all the characters, but now you're just a secondary character. This is the story of your mother's life, and she is the one who is watching the movie with all her attention. Then you realize that your mother is not the same person who was in your movie. The way she projects herself is completely different in her movie. It's the way your mother wants everyone to perceive her. You know that it's not authentic. She's just acting. But then you begin to realize that it's the way she perceives *herself*, and it's kind of a shock.

Then you notice that the character who has your face is not the same person who was in your movie. You say to yourself, "Ah, this isn't me," but now you can see how your mother perceives you, what she believes about you, and it's far from what you believe about yourself. Then you see the character of your father, the way your mother perceives him, and it's not at all the way you perceive him. It's completely distorted, and so is her perception of all the other characters. You see the way your mother perceives your beloved, and you even get a little upset with your mom. "How dare she!" You stand up and get out of there.

You go to the next theater, and it's the story of your beloved. Now you can see the way your beloved perceives you, and the character is completely different from the one who was in your movie and the one who was in your mother's movie. You can see the way your beloved perceives your children, your family, your friends. You can see the way your beloved wants to project him- or herself, and it's not the way you perceive your beloved at all. Then you decide to leave that movie, and go to your children's movie. You see the way your children see you, the way they see Grandpa, Grandma, and you can hardly believe it. Then you watch the movies of your brothers and sisters, of your friends, and you find out that everybody is distorting all the characters in their movie.

After seeing all these movies, you decide to return to the first theater to see your own movie once again. You look at yourself acting in your movie, but you no longer believe anything you're watching; you no longer believe your own story because you can see that it's just a story. Now you know that all the acting you did your whole life was really for nothing because nobody perceives you the way you want to be perceived. You can see that all the drama that happens in your movie isn't really noticed by anybody around you. It's obvious that everybody's attention is focused on their own movie. They don't even notice when you're sitting right beside them in their theater! The actors have all their attention on their story, and that is the only reality they live in. Their attention is so hooked by their own creation that they don't even notice their *own* presence — the one who is observing their movie.

In that moment, everything changes for you. Nothing is the same anymore, because now you see what's really happening. People live in their own world, in their own movie, in their own story. They invest all their faith in that story, and that story is truth for them, but it's a relative truth, because it's not truth for you. Now you can see that all their opinions about you really concern the character who lives in their movie, not in yours. The one who they are judging in your name is a character they create. Whatever people think of you is really about the *image* they have of you, and that image isn't you.

At this point, it's clear that the people you love the most don't really know you, and you don't know them either. The only thing you know about them is what you believe about them. You only know the image you created for them, and that image has nothing to do with the real people. You thought that you knew your parents, your spouse, your children, and your friends very well. The truth is you have no idea what is going on in their world — what they are thinking, what they are feeling, what they are dreaming. What is even more surprising is that you thought you knew *yourself*. Then you come to the conclusion that you don't even know yourself, because you've been acting for so long that you've mastered pretending to be what you are not.

With this awareness, you realize how ridiculous it is to say, "My beloved doesn't understand me. Nobody understands me." Of course they don't. You don't even understand yourself. Your personality is always changing from one moment to the next, according to the role you are playing, according to the secondary characters in your story, according to the way you are dreaming at that time. At home, you have a certain personality. At work, your personality is completely different. With your female friends, it's one way; with your male friends, it's another way. But all your life you made the assumption that other people knew you so well, and when they didn't do what you expected them to do, you took it personally, reacted with anger, and used the word to create a lot of conflict and drama for nothing.

Now it's easy to understand why there is so much conflict between humans. The world is populated by billions of dreamers who aren't aware that people are living in their own world, dreaming their own dream. From the point of view of the main character, which is their *only* point of view, everything is all about them. When the secondary characters say something that doesn't agree with their point of view, they get angry, and try to defend their position. They want the secondary characters to be the way they want them to be, and if they are not, they feel very hurt. They take *everything* personally. With this awareness, you can also understand the solution, and it's something so simple and logical: *Don't take anything personally.*

Now the meaning of the second agreement is profoundly clear. This agreement gives you immunity in the interaction you have with the secondary characters in your story. You don't have to concern yourself with other people's points of view. Once you can see that nothing others say or do is about you, it doesn't matter who gossips about you, who blames you, who rejects you, who disagrees with your point of view. All the gossip doesn't affect you. You don't even bother to defend your point of view. You just let the dogs bark, and surely they will bark, and bark, and bark. So what? Whatever people say doesn't affect you because you are immune to their opinions and their emotional poison. You are immune from the predators, the ones who use gossip to hurt other people, the ones who want to use other people to hurt themselves.

Don't take anything personally is a beautiful tool of interaction with your own kind, human to human. And it's a big ticket to personal freedom because you no longer have to rule your life according to other people's opinions. This really frees you! You can do whatever you want to do, knowing that whatever you do has nothing to do with anyone but you.

The only person who needs to be concerned about the story of you is *you*. This awareness changes everything. Remember, awareness of the truth is the first step to self-mastery, and that is what you're doing right now. You're being reminded of the truth.

Now that you understand this truth, now that you are aware, how can you take anything personally anymore? Once you understand that all humans live in their own world, in their own movie, in their own dream, the second agreement is pure common sense: *Don't take anything personally.*

5

TRUTH OR FICTION

The Third Agreement:
Don't Make Assumptions

FOR CENTURIES, EVEN MILLENNIA, HUMANS HAVE believed that a conflict exists in the human mind— a conflict between good and evil. But this isn't true. Good and evil are just the result of the conflict, because the *real* conflict is between the truth and lies. Perhaps we should say that *all* conflict is the result of lies, because the truth has no conflict at all. The truth doesn't need to prove itself; it exists whether we believe in it or not. Lies only exist if we create them, and they only survive if we believe in them. Lies are just a distortion of the word, a distortion of the meaning of a message, and that distortion is in the reflection, the human mind. Lies aren't real — they're our creation — but we give them life and make them real in the virtual reality of our mind.

When I was a teenager, my grandfather told me this simple truth, but it took years for me to really understand it because I was always thinking, "How can we know the truth?" I was using symbols to try to understand the truth, when the real truth is that the symbols have nothing to say about the truth. The truth existed long before humans created symbols.

As artists, we're always distorting the truth with symbols, but that's not the problem. As we said before, the problem is when we *believe* that distortion, because some lies are innocent, and others are deadly. Let's consider how we can use the word to create a story, a *superstition*, about a chair. What do we know about a chair? We can say that a chair is made of wood, or metal, or cloth, but we're just using symbols to express a point of view. The truth is that we don't really know what the object is. But we can use the word with all of our authority to deliver a message to ourselves and to everyone around us: "This chair is ugly. I hate this chair."

The message is already distorted, but this is just the beginning. We can say, "It's a stupid chair, and I think that whoever sits in the chair might become stupid also. I think we have to destroy the chair because if someone sits in the chair and it falls apart, that person will fall and break a hip. Oh yes, the chair is evil! Let's create a law against the chair so that everybody knows that it's a danger to society. From now on, it's prohibited to get near the evil chair!"

If we deliver this message, then whoever receives the message and agrees with the message starts to become afraid of the evil chair. Very soon, there are people who are so afraid of the chair that they start having nightmares about it. They become obsessed with the evil chair, and of course they have to destroy the chair before it destroys them.

Do you see what we can do with the word? The chair is just an object. It exists, and that's the truth. But the story we create about the chair is not the truth; it's a superstition. It's a distorted message, and that message is the lie. If we don't believe the lie, no problem. If we believe the lie and try to impose that lie on other people, it can lead to what we call *evil*. Of course, what we call *evil* has many levels, depending on our personal power. Some people can lead the whole world into a great war where millions of people die. There are tyrants all around the world who invade other countries and destroy their people because the tyrants believe in lies.

Now we can easily understand why there is a conflict in the human mind, and only in the *human* mind — the virtual reality — because it doesn't exist in the rest of nature. There are billions of humans who distort all those symbols in their heads and deliver distorted messages. That's what really happened to humanity. I think that answers why all the wars exist, why all the injustice and abuse exist, why the dream that we call *hell* exists in the world of humans. Hell is nothing but a dream full of lies.

Remember, our dream is controlled by what we believe, and what we believe could be truth, or could be fiction. The truth leads us to our authenticity, to happiness. Lies lead us to limitations in our lives, to suffering and drama. Whoever believes in truth, lives in heaven. Whoever believes in lies, sooner or later lives in hell. We don't have to die to go to heaven or hell. Heaven is all around us, just as hell is all around us. Heaven is a point of view, a state of mind, and so is hell. It's obvious that lies have been running every show in our head. Humans create the lies, and then the lies control the humans. But sooner or later the truth arrives, and the lies cannot survive the presence of the truth.

Centuries ago, people believed that the earth was flat. Some said that elephants were supporting the earth, and that made them feel safe. "Good, now we know that the earth is flat." Well, now we know that it isn't flat! The belief that the earth was flat was considered the truth, and almost everybody agreed, but did that make it true?

One of the biggest lies we hear at the present time is: "Nobody's perfect." It's a great excuse for our behavior, and almost everybody agrees, but is it true? On the contrary, every human in this world is perfect, but we've been hearing this lie since we were children, and as a consequence, we keep judging ourselves against an *image* of perfection. We keep searching for perfection, and in our search we find that everything in the universe is perfect except the humans. The sun is perfect, the stars are perfect, the planets are perfect, but when it comes to the humans, "Nobody's perfect." The truth is that everything in creation is perfect, including the humans.

If we don't have the awareness to see this truth, it's because we are blinded by the lie. You may say, "What about someone who is physically disabled?

Is that person perfect?" Well, according to what you know, that person may be imperfect, but is what you know the truth? Who says that what we call a *disability* or even a *disease* isn't perfect?

Everything about us is perfect, including any disability or disease that we may have. Someone with a learning difficulty is perfect; someone born without a finger or an arm or an ear is perfect; someone with a disease is perfect. Only perfection exists, and that awareness is another important step in our evolution. To say otherwise is not to have the awareness of what we are. And it's not enough to *say* that we're perfect; we need to *believe* that we're perfect. If we believe ourselves to be imperfect, that lie gathers more lies for support, and together all those lies repress the truth and guide the dream that we're creating for ourselves. Lies are nothing but superstitions, and I can assure you that we live in a world of superstition. But again, are we aware of it?

Just imagine waking up tomorrow morning in fourteenth-century Europe, knowing what you presently know, believing what you believe today. Imagine what those people would think of you, how they would judge you. They would put you on trial for taking a bath every day. Everything you believe would threaten what they believe. How long would it take before they accused you of being a witch? They would torture you, make you confess to being a witch, and finally kill you because of their fear of your beliefs. You can easily see that those people lived their lives immersed in superstition. Hardly anything they believed was true, and you can easily see that because of what you believe today. But those people were not aware of their superstitions. Their way of life was completely normal for them; they didn't know any better because they never learned anything else.

Then perhaps what you believe about yourself is just as full of superstition as the beliefs of those people long ago. Just imagine if humans from seven or eight centuries in the future could see what most of us believe about ourselves today. The way that most of us relate to our own body is still barbarian, though not as much as seven hundred years ago. Our body is completely loyal to us, but we judge our body and abuse our body; we treat it as if it's the enemy when it's our ally. Our society places a lot of importance on being attractive according to the images we see in the media — on television, in movies, in fashion magazines. If we believe that we are not attractive enough according to these images, then we believe a lie, and we are using the word against ourselves, against the truth.

The people in control of the media tell us what to believe, how to dress, what to eat, and they manipulate humans like puppets, which means in whatever way they want. If they want us to hate someone, they spread gossip all around, and the lies work their magic. When we stop being puppets, it's obvious that our lives have been guided by lies and superstitions. Imagine what future humans would think of our superstitions. If they believed in the perfection of everything in creation, including every human, would we crucify them for their beliefs?

What is the truth and what is the lie? Once again, awareness is so important, because the truth doesn't come with words, with knowledge. But lies do, and there are billions of lies. Humans believe so many lies because we aren't aware. We ignore the truth or we just don't see the truth. When we are domesticated, we accumulate a lot of knowledge, and all that knowledge is just like a wall of fog that doesn't allow us to perceive the truth, what really *is*. We only see what we want to see; we only hear what we want to hear. Our belief system is just like a mirror that only shows us what we believe.

In our development, as we grow throughout our lives, we learn so many lies that the whole structure of our lies becomes very complicated. And we make it even more complicated because we *think*, and we *believe* in what we think. We make the assumption that what we believe is the absolute truth, and we never stop to consider that our truth is a relative truth, a virtual truth. Usually, it's not even close to any kind of truth, but it's the closest we can get without awareness.

THE THIRD AGREEMENT: DON'T MAKE ASSUMPTIONS

This takes us to the third agreement: *Don't make assumptions*. Making assumptions is just looking for trouble, because most assumptions are not the truth; they're fiction. One big assumption we make is that everything in our virtual reality is the truth. Another big assumption we make is that everything in everyone else's virtual reality is the truth. Well, now you know that none of the virtual realities are the truth!

Using our awareness, we can easily see all the assumptions we make, and we can see how easy it is to make them. Humans have a powerful imagination, very powerful, and there are so many ideas and stories that we can imagine. We listen to the symbols talking in our head. We start imagining what other people are doing, what they're thinking, what they're saying about us, and we dream things up in our imagination. We invent a whole story that's only truth for us, but we believe it. One assumption leads to another assumption; we jump to conclusions, and we take our story very personally. Then we blame other people, and we usually start gossiping to try to justify our assumptions. Of course, by gossiping, a distorted message becomes even more distorted.

Making assumptions and then taking them personally is the beginning of hell in this world. Almost all of our conflicts are based on this, and it's easy to understand why. Assumptions are nothing more than lies that we are telling ourselves. This creates a big drama for nothing, because we don't really know if something is true or not. Making assumptions is just looking for drama when there's no drama happening. And if drama is happening in someone else's story, so what? It's not your story; it's someone else's story.

Be aware that almost everything you tell yourself is an assumption. If you're a parent, you know how easy it is to make assumptions about your children. It's midnight, and your daughter isn't home yet. She went out to dance, and you thought she would be home by now. You start imagining the worst; you start making assumptions: "Oh, what if something happened to her? Maybe I should call the police." There are so many things you can imagine, and you create a whole drama of possibilities in your head. Ten minutes later your daughter arrives home with a big smile. When the truth arrives and all the lies are dispelled, you realize that you were simply torturing yourself for nothing. *Don't make assumptions.*

If not taking anything personally gives you immunity in the interaction that you have with other people, then not making assumptions gives you immunity in the interaction that you have with yourself, with your voice of knowledge, or what we call *thinking.* Making assumptions is all about thinking. We think too much, and thinking leads to assumptions. Just thinking "What if?" can create a huge drama in our lives. Every human can think a lot, and thinking brings fear. We have no control over all that thinking, all those symbols that we distort in our head. If we just stop thinking, we no longer try to explain anything to ourselves, and this keeps us from making assumptions.

Humans have a need to explain and justify everything; we have a need for knowledge, and we make assumptions to fulfill our need to *know*. We don't care whether the knowledge is true or not. Truth or fiction, we believe 100 percent in what we believe, and we go on believing it, because just having knowledge makes us feel safe. There are so many things that the mind cannot explain; we have all these questions that need answers. But instead of asking questions when we don't know something, we make all sorts of assumptions. If we just ask questions, we won't have to make assumptions. It's always better to ask and be clear.

If we don't make assumptions, we can focus our attention on the truth, not on what we *think* is the truth. Then we see life the way it is, not the way we want to see it. As we shall see, when we don't believe our own assumptions, the power of our belief that we invested in them returns to us. When we recover all the energy that we invested in making assumptions, we can use that energy to create a new dream: our personal heaven. *Don't make assumptions.*

6

THE POWER OF BELIEF

The Symbol of Santa Claus

THERE WAS A TIME IN YOUR LIFE WHEN YOU completely owned the power of your belief, but when you were educated to be a part of humanity, the power of your belief went into all those symbols that you learned, and at a certain point the symbols gained power over you. In truth, the power of your belief went into *everything* that you know, and since then everything that you know has ruled your life. Obviously, when we are little children, we are overcome by the power of everyone else's beliefs. The symbols are a wonderful invention, but we are introduced to the symbols with the opinions and beliefs already there. We ingest every opinion without questioning if it's truth or not. And the problem is that by the time we master a language with all the opinions that we hear growing up, the symbols already have the power of our belief.

This isn't good or bad or right or wrong. It's just the way it is, and it happens to all of us. We are learning to be a member of our society. We learn a language, we learn a religion or philosophy, we learn a way of being, and we structure our whole belief system based on everything we are told. We have no reason to doubt what other people tell us until the first heartbreak happens, and we find out that something they told us isn't true.

We go to school, and we hear older kids talking. Referring to us, they say, "You see that kid? He still believes in Santa Claus." Sooner or later, we find out that Santa Claus doesn't exist. Can you remember your reaction, how you *felt* when you found out that Santa Claus was not the truth? I don't think your parents had bad intentions. Believing in Santa Claus is a wonderful tradition for millions of people. The lyrics of one song describe what we're told about the symbol we know as *Santa*: "You better watch out, you better not cry, you better not pout, I'm telling you why. Santa Claus is coming to town!" We're told that Santa knows everything we do or don't do; he knows when we've been bad or good; he knows when we don't brush our teeth. And we *believe* this.

Christmas comes, and we see a huge difference in the gifts that children receive. Let's say you ask Santa for a bicycle and you were good the whole year. Your family is very poor. You open your gifts, and you don't receive a bicycle. Your neighbor, who was very bad — and you know what *very bad* means — receives a bicycle. You say, "I was good, this boy was bad, how come I didn't receive a bicycle? If Santa Claus really knows everything that I do, for sure he knows everything that my neighbor did. Why would Santa bring a bicycle to my neighbor and not to me?"

It's just not fair, and you don't understand why. Your emotional reaction is envy, anger, even sadness. You see the other little guy riding his bicycle very happily all around, behaving worse than he did before, and you want to go and hit him or break the bicycle. *Injustice*. And that sense of injustice is because you believe in a lie. It's an innocent lie, with no bad intention, of course, but you *believe* it, and you make an agreement with yourself: "From now on, I won't be good. I'm going to be bad, like my neighbor." Later, you discover that Santa Claus is not true; he isn't real. But it's too late. You already released all the emotional poison; you already suffered the anger, the jealousy, the sadness. You already suffered from making an agreement that was based on a lie.

This is just one example of how we invest our faith in a symbol. There are hundreds, even thousands, of symbols, stories, and superstitions that we learn.

The symbol of Santa Claus demonstrates how even believing in an innocent lie can bring up emotions that feel like a fire burning inside us. They feel like poison —they're hurting us, they're hurting our body — and we suffer from a story that isn't real. The emotions are real; they are part of the truth, but the reason we are feeling them is not real. It's not truth; it's fiction.

If you're asking yourself why you're so miserable at times, it's because you're telling yourself a story that isn't true, but you believe it. The truth is that your dream has become distorted, but that's not good or bad or right or wrong, because it's happening to billions of other people. You're not the only one in that situation, and that's the good news.

The world of the symbols is extremely powerful because we make every symbol powerful with that force that comes from deep inside us — that force that we call *life*, *faith*, or *intent*. We don't even realize that it's happening, but together all of the symbols form a whole structure made by agreements, and we call it a *belief system*. From a single letter to a word, from a single story to an entire philosophy, everything we agree to believe goes into that structure.

The belief system gives form and structure to our virtual reality, and with every agreement we make, the structure grows stronger and gains more power until it becomes nearly as rigid as a brick building. If we imagine every symbol, every concept, every agreement as a brick, then our faith is the mortar that holds the bricks together. As we continue to learn throughout our lives, we mix the symbols in many directions, and the concepts interact with themselves to create more complex concepts. The abstract mind becomes organized in a more complicated way, and the structure keeps growing and growing, until we have a totality of everything that we know.

This structure is what the Toltec call the *human form*. The human form is not the form of the physical body; it's the form that our mind takes. It's the structure of our beliefs about ourselves, about everything that helps us make sense of our dream. The human form gives us our identity, but it's not the same as the frame of the dream. The frame of the dream is the material world as it is, which is truth. The human form is the belief system with all the elements of judgment. Everything in that belief system is our personal truth, and we judge everything according to those beliefs, even if those beliefs go against our own inner nature.

In the process of domestication, the belief system becomes the *book of law* that rules our lives. When we follow the rules according to our book of law, we reward ourselves; when we don't follow the rules, we punish ourselves. The belief system becomes the big judge in our mind, and also the greatest victim because first it judges us, then it punishes us. The big judge is made by symbols, and it works with symbols to judge everything we perceive, including the symbols! The victim is the part of us that receives the judgment and suffers the punishment. And when we interact with the outside dream, we judge and punish everyone and everything else according to our personal book of law.

The big judge is doing a perfect job, of course, because we agree with all those laws. The problem is that the belief system comes to life within us, and uses our knowledge against us. It uses everything we know, all of our rules about how we have to live our lives, to punish the victim, which is the human. It uses our language to create the self-judgment, the self-rejection, the guilt, the shame. It verbally abuses us and makes us miserable by creating our personal demons and our personal dream of hell. There are so many symbols that we can use to say the same thing.

The belief system rules the human life like a tyrant. It takes our freedom away from us and makes us its slave. It takes power over the *real* us, the human life, and it isn't even real! The real us stays hidden someplace in the mind, and the one who controls the mind at that point is everything we know, everything we agreed to believe. The human body, which is beautiful and perfect, becomes the victim of all the judgment and punishment; it becomes just a vehicle where the mind acts and projects itself through the body.

The belief system is in the realm of the mind; we cannot see it or measure it, but we know that it exists.

Perhaps what we don't know is that this structure only exists because we create it. Our creation is completely attached to us; it follows us wherever we go. We've been living this way for so long that we don't even notice that we live in this structure. And even though the mind isn't real — it's virtual — it's also *total power* because it's also created by life.

Then something very important in the mastery of awareness is to be aware of our own creation, to be aware that it's alive. Every one of our beliefs, from a minimal one like the sound of a letter to a whole philosophy, is using our life force to survive. If we could see our mind in action, we would see millions of life forms, and we would see that we are giving life to our creation by giving it the power of our faith, by giving it all of our attention. We are using our life force to support the whole structure. Without us, these ideas could not exist; without us, the whole structure would collapse.

If we use the power of our imagination, we can see the creation of our "personal mythology," the construction of our belief system, and the beginning of investing our faith in lies. In the process of all that construction — all that learning we do — there are many concepts that contradict other concepts. There are so many different dreams that we build, and when we create so many structures, they go against one another and annul the power of our word. In that moment, our word is almost nothing, because when there are two forces going in opposite directions, the result is zero. When there is only one force going in one direction, the power is immense, and our intentions manifest just because we say so, just because our word has all the power of our faith.

As children, we invest our faith in almost everything that we learn, and this is how we lose power over our own lives. By the time we grow up, our faith is already invested in so many lies that we hardly have any power left to create the dream that we want to create. The belief system has all the power of our faith, and by the end of the equation we remain with almost zero faith, zero power. And it's easy to see how we invest our faith in a symbol like Santa Claus, but it's not as easy to see how we do the very same thing with every symbol, every story, and every opinion that we learn about ourselves, about everything.

I think this is very important to understand, and the only way to understand it is by being aware that this is what we are doing. If we have the awareness that we invest our personal power in everything that we believe, perhaps it will be easy to take our power back from the symbols, and those symbols will no longer have any power over us. If we take the power out of every symbol, the symbols become just symbols. Then they will obey the creator, which means the *real* us, and they will serve their *real* purpose: to be a tool that we can use to communicate.

When we find out that Santa Claus isn't the truth, we no longer believe in Santa Claus, and the power we invested in that symbol returns to us. This is when we become aware that we are the one who agreed to believe in Santa Claus. When we recover our awareness, we can see that we are the one who agreed to believe in the entire symbology. And if we are the one who put the power of our faith in every symbol, then we are the only one who can take that power back.

If we have this awareness, I think we can recover the power over everything that we believe and never lose control over our own creation. Once we can see that we are the one who creates the structure of our beliefs, this helps us to recover faith in ourselves. When we have faith in ourselves instead of the belief system, we have no doubt where that power comes from, and we start to dismantle the structure.

Once the structure of our belief system is no longer there, we become very flexible. We can create anything we want to create; we can do anything we want to do. We can invest our faith in anything we want to believe. It's our choice. If we no longer believe in all that we know that makes us suffer, then just like magic, our suffering disappears. And we don't need a lot of thinking; we need action. It's action that is going to make the difference.

7

PRACTICE MAKES THE MASTER

The Fourth Agreement:
Always Do Your Best

WHEN YOU ARE READY TO CHANGE YOUR LIFE, when you are ready to change your agreements, the most important thing is awareness. You cannot change your agreements if you aren't aware of what you like and what you don't like. How can you change anything if you are not even aware of what you want to change? But it's more than just being aware. It's the practice that will make a difference, because you can be aware, but that doesn't mean your life will change. Change is the result of action; it's the result of practice. Practice makes the master.

Everything you have ever learned, you learned through repetition and practice. You learned to talk, you learned to walk, you even learned to write by repetition. You are a master of speaking your language because you practiced. This is the same way that you learned all the beliefs that rule your life: by practice. The way you are living your life right now is the result of many years of practice.

During your whole life you practiced every moment to become what you believe you are right now. You practiced until it became automatic. And when you start practicing something new, when you change what you believe you are, your whole life is going to change. If you practice being *impeccable with your word*, if you *don't take anything personally*, if you *don't make assumptions*, you are going to break thousands of agreements that keep you trapped in the dream of hell. Very soon, what you agree to believe will become the choice of your *authentic* self, not the choice of the *image* of yourself that you thought you were.

The first agreement, *be impeccable with your word,* is all you need to create a beautiful life. It will take you all the way to heaven, but you may need support for this agreement. When you *don't take anything personally,* when you *don't make assumptions,* you can imagine that it's easier to be impeccable with your word. When you don't make assumptions, it's easier not to take anything personally, and vice versa. By not taking anything personally, and by not making assumptions, you are supporting the first agreement.

The first three agreements may seem difficult to do. They may even seem impossible for us to do. Well, believe me, it's not impossible, but I have to agree that it's difficult, because we practice exactly the opposite. All our lives we practice believing the voice in our head. But there is the fourth agreement, and it's easy. This is the agreement that makes everything possible: *Always do your best.* You can do your best, and that's it. No more, no less. Just do your best. *Do.* Take action. How can you do your best if you don't take action?

Always do your best is the agreement that everybody can do. Your best is, in fact, the only thing you *can* do. And the best you can do doesn't mean that sometimes you give 80 percent and other times you just give 20 percent. You're always giving 100 percent — that's always your intention — it's just that your best is always changing. From one moment to the next, you are never the same. You are alive and changing all the time, and your best is also changing from one moment to the next.

Your best will depend on whether you are feeling physically tired or refreshed. Your best will depend on how you are feeling emotionally. Your best is going to change over time, and as you form the habit of practicing the Four Agreements, your best is going to get better.

The fourth agreement allows the first three agreements to become deeply ingrained habits. Repetition and practice will make you the master, but don't expect that you can master these agreements right away. Don't expect that you are always going to be impeccable with your word, or that you are never going to take anything personally, or that you are never going to make assumptions. Your habits are too strong and firmly rooted in your mind. Just do your best.

If you fail to keep one of the agreements, make the agreement again. Begin again tomorrow, and again the next day. Keep practicing and practicing. Each day will become easier. By doing your best, the habits of misusing your word, taking things personally, and making assumptions will become weaker and less frequent over time. If you keep taking action to change your habits, it's going to happen.

Eventually the moment will come when all four agreements become a habit. You don't even try. It's automatic. It's effortless. One day you discover that you are ruling your life with the Four Agreements. Can you imagine your life when these agreements become a habit? Instead of struggling with conflict and drama, your whole life becomes very easy!

If you are going to create anyway, if you cannot avoid dreaming, then why not create a beautiful dream? You have a mind, you perceive light, you are going to dream. If you make the choice to not create anything, you are going to get bored, and the big judge will resist being bored. Then of course it's going to judge you according to what you believe. "Oh, you are lazy. You should be doing something with your life." Then why not dream well and really enjoy your dream? If you can believe in your limitations, then why not believe in the beauty and power of life that's flowing through you?

Life gives us everything, and everything in life can be a pleasure. Why not believe in the generosity of life? Why not learn to be generous and kind to yourself? If that makes you happy, and you're good to everybody around you, why not? If you're always transforming — if your dream is always changing even if you don't want it to change — why not master the transformation and create your personal heaven?

The dream of your life is made by thousands of little dreams that are dynamic. Dreams are born, they grow, and they die, which means they're always transforming. But usually they're transforming without your awareness. Once you are aware that you're dreaming, you recover your power to change the dream whenever you choose. When you discover that you have the power to create a dream of heaven, you want to change your dream, and the Four Agreements are the perfect tool for that. They challenge the tyrant, the judge, and the victim in your head. They challenge all those tiny agreements that make your life difficult.

And if you challenge your beliefs just by asking yourself if what you believe is true, you may find out something very interesting: All your life you tried to be good enough for somebody else, and you left yourself last. You sacrificed your personal freedom to live according to somebody else's point of view. You tried to be good enough for your mother, your father, your teachers, your beloved, your children, your religion, and society. After trying for so many years, you try to be good enough for *yourself*, and you find out that you're not good enough for yourself.

Why not put yourself first, maybe for the first time in your life? You can relearn how to love yourself by accepting yourself, unconditionally. And you can start by projecting unconditional love to the *authentic* you. Then practice loving your authentic self more and more. When you love yourself unconditionally, you are no longer easy prey for an outside predator who wants to control your life. You no longer sacrifice yourself for anyone. If you practice self-love, you will master self-love.

Always do your best is the agreement that helps you to become the master artist. The first three agreements are in the realm of the virtual reality. The fourth agreement is in the realm of the physical. It's about taking action and practicing, and practicing, until you become a dream master. By doing your best, over and over, eventually you are going to master the art of transformation. The mastery of transformation is the second mastery of the artist, which you can clearly see in the fourth agreement. When you always do your best, you're taking action, you're transforming yourself, you're changing the dream of your life.

The goal of the second mastery is to face what you believe, and to transform what you believe. The mastery is achieved by changing your agreements, and reprogramming your own mind in your own way. The result you want is the freedom to live your own life instead of the life of the belief system. When that book of law is no longer in your mind, the tyrant, the judge, and the victim are no longer in your mind either.

The transformation has already started, and it always begins with you. Do you have the courage to be completely honest with yourself, to see the truth about how you write your story? Do you have the courage to see your superstitions and lies? Do you have the courage to review what you believe you are, or are there too many wounds to see? Perhaps you're thinking, "I don't know." But you're taking the challenge. You're transforming your dream, and it's happening right now because what you're doing is unlearning all your lies.

The Four Agreements are actually a summary of *the mastery of transformation*, and the mastery of transformation is the process of unlearning what you have already learned. You learn by making agreements, and you unlearn by breaking agreements. Every time you break an agreement, the power of faith that you invested in that agreement comes back to you because you no longer need to spend your energy to keep that agreement alive.

You start by breaking agreements that are small and require less power. As you unlearn, you begin to dismantle the structure of your knowledge, and this frees your faith. As you recover your faith, your personal power increases; your will becomes stronger.

This gives you the power to change another agreement, and then another, and another. Your personal power keeps growing and growing, and because you're much more powerful, you find that almost anything is possible. Soon you are making agreements that lead you to happiness, to joy, to love. Then these new agreements come alive and begin to interact with the outside world, and your whole dream changes.

When you unlearn, which is what you're doing now, you begin by facing what you believe. How are you going to face what you believe? You only have one tool to do this, and that tool is doubt. Doubt is a symbol, of course, but what it means is very powerful. With the power of doubt, you challenge every message you deliver and receive. You challenge every belief in your book of law. Then you challenge all the beliefs that rule society, until you break the spell of all the lies and superstitions that control your world. As you shall see in Part II, the fifth agreement gives you the power of doubt.

Part II

⚜

The Power of Doubt

8

THE POWER OF DOUBT

The Fifth Agreement:
Be Skeptical, but Learn to Listen

THE FIFTH AGREEMENT IS *BE SKEPTICAL, BUT LEARN to listen*. *Be skeptical* because most of what you hear isn't true. You know that humans speak with symbols, and that symbols aren't the truth. Symbols are only the truth because we agree, not because they are *really* the truth. But the second half of the agreement is *learn to listen*, and the reason is simple: When you learn to listen, you understand the meaning of the symbols that people are using; you understand their story, and the communication improves a lot. Then perhaps instead of all the confusion among humans who inhabit the earth, there will be clarity.

Once you realize that hardly anything you know through symbols is true, then *be skeptical* has a much bigger meaning. *Be skeptical* is masterful because it uses the power of doubt to discern the truth. Whenever you hear a message from yourself, or from another artist, simply ask: *Is it truth, or is it not truth? Is it reality or is it a virtual reality?* The doubt takes you *behind* the symbols, and makes you responsible for every message you deliver and receive. Why would you want to invest your faith in any message that is not true? By being skeptical, you don't believe every message; you don't put your faith in symbols, and when your faith is not in symbols, your faith is in yourself.

Then if faith is believing without a doubt, and doubt is not believing, *be skeptical. Don't believe.* And what will you not believe? Well, you will not believe all the stories that we artists create with our knowledge. You know that most of our knowledge isn't true — the whole symbology isn't true — so *don't believe me, don't believe yourself,* and *don't believe anybody else.* The truth doesn't need you to believe it; the truth simply is, and it survives whether you believe it or not. Lies need you to believe them. If you don't believe lies, they don't survive your skepticism, and they simply disappear.

But skepticism can go in two directions. One way is to pretend to be skeptical because you think you're too smart to be gullible. "Look at how intelligent I am. I don't believe in anything." This is not skepticism. To be skeptical is not to believe everything you hear, and you don't believe because it's not the truth, that's all. The way to be skeptical is just to be aware that the entire humanity believes in lies. You know that humans distort the truth because we are dreaming, and our dream is just a reflection of the truth.

Every artist distorts the truth, but you don't need to judge what somebody says, or call that person a liar. All of us tell lies in one way or another, and it's not because we want to lie. It's because of what we believe; it's because of the symbols we learned, and the way we are applying all of those symbols. Once you are aware of this, the fifth agreement makes a lot of sense, and it can make a very big difference in your life.

People will come to you and tell you their personal story. They will tell you their point of view, what they believe is truth. But you won't judge if it's truth or if it's not truth. You don't have any judgment, but you do have respect. You listen to the way other people express their symbols, knowing that whatever they say is distorted by their beliefs. You know that what they are telling you is nothing but a story, and you know that because you can feel it. You just *know*. But you also know when their words come from truth, and you know without words, and that's the main point.

Truth or fiction, you don't have to believe any-one's story. You don't have to form an opinion about what someone says. You don't have to express your own opinion. You don't have to agree or disagree. Just *listen*. The more impeccable a person is with the word, the clearer the message will be, but the words that come from another artist have nothing to do with you. You know that it's nothing personal. You listen and you understand all the words, but the words no longer affect you. You no longer judge what other people say because you understand what they are doing. They are only letting you know what is going on in their virtual world.

You already have the awareness that all artists live in their own dream, in their own world. In that world, whatever they perceive is truth for them, and it could be that it's absolutely true for the artists who are expressing their story, but it's not truth for you. The only truth for you is what you perceive in your world. With this awareness, there's nothing to prove to anyone. It's not about being right or wrong. You respect whatever somebody says because it's another artist speaking. Respect is so important. When you learn to listen, you show respect for the other artists — you show respect for their art, for their creation.

All artists have the right to create their art in whatever way they want. They have the right to believe whatever they want to believe; they have the right to say whatever they have to say, but if you don't learn to listen, you will never understand what they're saying. Listening is so important in communication. When you learn to listen, you know exactly what other people want. Once you know what they want, what you do with that information is up to you. You can react or not react, you can agree or disagree with what they say, and that depends on what *you* want.

Just because other people want something, that doesn't mean you have to give them what they want. People are always trying to hook your attention, because through the attention they can download any information. Many times you just don't want that information. You listen; you don't want it, you ignore it and change directions. But if that information hooks your attention, then you really want to listen to find out if what someone is saying is important to you. Then you can share your point of view if you want to, knowing that it's just a point of view. That's your choice, but the key is to *listen*.

If you don't learn to listen, you will never understand what I am sharing with you right now. You will jump to conclusions, and react like it's your dream, when it's not your dream. When other artists are sharing their dream with you, just be aware that it's *their* dream. You know what your dream is, and what your dream is not.

Right now, I'm sharing the way that I perceive the world, the way that I dream, and my stories are truth for me, but I know they are not the *real* truth, so don't believe me. Whatever I tell you is just my point of view. Of course, from my point of view,

I'm sharing the truth with you. I do my best to use words in the most impeccable way so that you can understand what I'm saying, but even if I share an exact copy of the truth with you, I know that you will distort my message as soon as it goes from my mind into yours. You will hear the message, and tell yourself the same message in a completely different way, according to *your* point of view.

Then perhaps what I say is the truth or not the truth, but perhaps what you believe is not the truth. I am only one half of the message; you are the other half. I am responsible for what I say, but I am not responsible for what you understand. You are responsible for what you understand; you are responsible for whatever you do with what you hear in your head, because you are the one who gives the meaning to every word that you hear.

Right now, you are interpreting what I'm saying according to your personal knowledge. You are rearranging the symbols and transforming them in a way that maintains an equilibrium with everything in your belief system. Once you achieve that equilibrium, you may or may not accept my story as the truth. And you can make the assumption that what you are telling yourself is what I intended to say, but it doesn't mean that your assumption is true. You can misinterpret what I say. You can use what you hear to blame me, to blame somebody else, to blame yourself, to blame your religion or philosophy, to be angry with everybody, mainly with yourself. You can also use what you hear to find the truth, to find yourself, to make peace with yourself, and perhaps to change the message that you deliver to yourself.

Whatever you do with my words is up to you. It's your dream, and I respect your dream. You don't have to believe me, but if you learn to listen, you can understand what I'm saying, and if the information I'm sharing with you makes sense to you, then you can make it a part of your dream if you want to. You can take whatever works for you and use it to modify your dream, and what doesn't work for you, just ignore. It won't make any difference to me, but it might make a difference to you, because I make the assumption, knowing that it's an assumption, that you want to become a better artist, and that's why you are challenging your own beliefs.

Then *be skeptical.* Don't believe me, don't believe anybody else, but especially don't believe yourself. When I say *don't believe yourself,* oh my goodness, can you see the implication? Don't believe everything you learned! Not believing yourself is a huge advantage, because most of what you learned is not the truth. Everything you know, your whole reality, is nothing but symbols. But you are not that bunch of symbols that talk in your head. You know that, and that's why you are skeptical and you don't believe yourself.

If your beliefs are telling you, "I'm fat. I'm ugly. I'm old. I'm a loser. I'm not good enough. I'm not strong enough. I'll never make it," then don't believe yourself, because it's not true. These messages are distorted. They're nothing but lies. Once you can see the lies, you don't have to believe them. Use the power of doubt to challenge every message that you deliver to yourself. "Is it *really* true that I'm ugly? Is it *really* true that I'm not good enough?" Is this message real, or is it virtual? Of course, it's virtual. None of these messages come from truth, from life; they come from distortions in our knowledge. The truth is, there are no ugly people. There is no good enough or strong enough. There's no universal book of law where any of these judgments are true. These judgments are just agreements that humans make.

Can you see the consequences of believing yourself? Believing yourself is one of the worst things you can do because you've been telling yourself lies your whole life, and if you believe all those lies, that's why your dream isn't a pleasant dream. If you believe what you tell yourself, you may use all those symbols that you learned to hurt yourself. Your personal dream may even be pure hell because believing in lies is how you create your own hell. If you're suffering, it's not because anybody is making you suffer; it's because you obey the tyrant that's ruling your head. When the tyrant obeys you, when there's no longer a judge or a victim in your mind, you won't be suffering any longer.

Your tyrant is ruthless. It's always abusing you by using all those symbols against you. It thrives on emotional poison generated by negative emotions, and the way it generates these emotions in you is by judging and giving opinions. Nobody judges you more than you judge yourself. Of course you try to escape from the judgment, the guilt, the rejection, the punishment. But how can you escape from your own thoughts? If you don't like someone, you can walk away. If you don't like yourself, wherever you go, you're still there. You can hide from everybody else, but you cannot hide from your own judgment. It seems as if there is no escape.

That's why so many people overeat, take drugs, abuse alcohol, and become addicted to various substances and behaviors. They try to do whatever they can to avoid their own story, to avoid their own creation that's distorting all those symbols in their head. Some people are suffering from so much emotional pain that they decide to take their own lives. That's what lies can do to any of us. The voice of knowledge can become so distorted and create so much self-hate that it kills the human. And all of this is just because we believe all those opinions that we learned over so many years.

Just imagine that all your own opinions, plus all the opinions of everybody around you, are like a huge hurricane inside you. Imagine believing all those opinions! Well, if you're skeptical, if you don't believe yourself, if you don't believe anybody else, then none of these opinions can disturb you or throw you off your center. When you have control over your own symbology, you are always centered, you are always relaxed and calm, because the *real* you makes the choices in your life, not the symbols. When you want to communicate something, you order the symbols, and that is the way they come out of your mouth.

You are the artist, and you can arrange the symbols in any way you want, in any direction you want, because all those symbols are at your command. You can use the symbols to ask for what you need, to express what you want, what you don't want. You can express your thoughts, your feelings, your dreams, in the most beautiful poetry or prose. But just because you use a language to communicate, it doesn't mean that you believe it. Why do you need to believe what you already know? When you are alone and talking to yourself, it's completely meaningless. What can you tell yourself that you don't already know?

If you understand the fifth agreement, you will see the reason why you don't need to believe what you can *see*, what you already know without words. The truth doesn't come with words. The truth is silent. It's something that you just know; it's something that you can feel without words, and it's called *silent knowledge*. Silent knowledge is what you know before you invest your faith in symbols. When you open yourself to the truth, and learn to listen, then all the symbols lose their value, and the only thing that remains is the truth. There's nothing to know; there's nothing to justify.

What I'm sharing with you isn't easy to understand, and at the same time, it's so simple that it's obvious. In the end, you are going to realize that languages are symbols that are only true because you *think* they are, and if you put them aside, what remains? The truth. Then you see a chair, and you won't know what to call it, but you can sit on it and the truth is there. Matter is truth. Life is truth. Light is truth. Love is truth. The human dream is not truth, but not being truth doesn't mean that it's bad. Being bad is just another concept that is not truth either.

Once you realize that you create the whole symbology to communicate with your own kind, then you find out that the symbols are not really good or bad or right or wrong. You make them right or you make them wrong with your beliefs. That is the power of your belief, but the truth is beyond belief. When you go beyond symbols, what you find is a world of perfection where everyone and everything in creation is perfect. Even the investment of your belief in every word is perfect. Even your anger, your drama, and your lies are perfect. Even the hell that you sometimes live in is perfect, because only perfection exists. Just imagine if you lived your whole life without learning all the lies in your knowledge, without suffering from investing your faith in lies, superstitions, and opinions. You would follow life like the rest of the animals, which means you would keep your innocence your entire life.

In the process of domestication, you lose your innocence, but in losing your innocence, you start to search for what you have lost, and this leads you to gain awareness. Once you recover awareness, you become completely responsible for your own evolution — for every choice you make in life.

When you are educated by the dream of the planet, you have no choice; you learn so many lies.

But maybe it's time to unlearn those lies, and relearn how to follow the truth by following your own heart. Unlearning, or what I call *undomestication*, is a very slow but powerful process. As we said before, every time you take your faith away from a symbol, that power comes back to you, and it keeps coming back to you, until finally the entire symbology has no power over you.

When you take away the power of every symbol and bring it back to you, the whole dream is powerless. And when all that power has returned to you, you are invincible. Nothing can defeat you. Or perhaps I should say that you can no longer defeat yourself, because it's exactly the same thing.

Once you recover all the power you invested in symbols, you don't believe every thought that comes into your head; you don't believe your own story. But you listen to your story, and because you respect your own story, you can enjoy it. When you go to the movies or read a novel, you don't believe it, but you can enjoy it, right? Once you can see the difference between reality and the virtual reality, you know that you can trust reality and you don't have to trust the virtual reality, but you can enjoy both. You can enjoy what is, and you can enjoy what you create.

Even though you know your story isn't true, you can create the most beautiful story, and you can guide your life through that story. You can create your personal heaven and live in that heaven. And if you can understand other people's stories, and they can understand yours, then together you can create the most beautiful dream. But first you need to unlearn a lot, and the fifth agreement is another perfect tool for that.

Wherever you go around the world, you will hear all kinds of opinions and stories from other people. You will find great storytellers wanting to tell you what you should do with your life: "You should do this, you should do that, you should do whatever." Don't believe them. *Be skeptical, but learn to listen* and then make your choices. Be responsible for every choice you make in your life. This is your life; it's nobody else's life, and you will find that it's nobody else's business what you do with your life.

For centuries, there have been people who claim to know the will of God, and who go around the world preaching goodness and rightness and condemning everybody. For centuries, there have been prophets who predicted big catastrophes in the world. Not that long ago, there were people who predicted that in the year 2000 all the computers would fail and society as we know it would disappear. Some people thought that we would return to the time of the caveman. The day arrived, we celebrated the new century, the new year, and what happened? Nothing happened.

Thousands of years ago, just like today, there were prophets who were waiting for the end of the world. At that time, a great master said, "There will be many false prophets who claim to be speaking the word of God. *Don't believe.*" You see, the fifth agreement is not really new. *Be skeptical, but learn to listen.*

9

THE DREAM OF THE FIRST ATTENTION

The Victims

THIS BRINGS ME TO THE STORY ABOUT ADAM AND Eve in Paradise. Adam and Eve represent all humans, and God told us that we could eat whatever we wanted except for the fruit of the Tree of Knowledge. The day that we eat the fruit of this tree, we would die. Well, we ate it, and we died.

Of course this is just a story, but the important thing is the meaning of this story. Why do we die when we eat the fruit of this tree? Because the real name for the Tree of Knowledge is the Tree of Death. The other tree in Paradise is the Tree of Life. Life is truth, and the truth just is, without words or symbols. The Tree of Knowledge is just a reflection of the Tree of Life. We already know that knowledge is created with symbols, and that symbols aren't real. When we eat the fruit of the Tree of Knowledge, the symbols become a virtual reality that talks to us as the voice of knowledge, and we live in that reality believing that it's real, which means without awareness, of course.

It's obvious that humans ate the fruit of the Tree of Death. From my point of view, there are billions of humans walking around in this world who are dead, but they don't *know* they are dead. Yes, their bodies are alive, but they are dreaming without any awareness that they are dreaming, and this is what the Toltec call *the dream of the first attention*.

The dream of the first attention is the dream that we create by using our attention for the very first time. This is what I also call *the ordinary dream of the humans*, or we can say that it's *the dream of the victims*, because we are victims of all the symbols that we create, we are victims of all the voices in our head, we are victims of all the superstitions and distortions in our knowledge. In the dream of the victims, where most people live, we are victimized by our religion, by our government, by our entire way of thinking and believing.

When we are children, we cannot defend ourselves against all the lies that come with the whole Tree of Knowledge. As we said before, our parents, schools, religion, and our entire society hook our attention and introduce us to their opinions and beliefs. We believe in the religion that we believe in because our parents believe in that religion, because they take us to church or another place of worship, and we learn to believe everything we are told. The adults who take care of us tell us their stories, and we go to school, and we hear more stories. We learn the story of our country; we learn about all the heroes, all the wars, all the human suffering.

The adults prepare us to be a part of our society, and I can say without a doubt that it's a society ruled completely by lies. We learn to live in the same dream they live in; our faith gets trapped in the structure of that dream, and that dream becomes normal for us. But I don't believe that they did this with any bad intention. The adults can only teach us what they know; they cannot teach us what they don't know. What they know is what they learned in their whole lives; it's what they believed in their whole lives. You can be sure that your parents did the best they could for you at the time. If they didn't do better, it's because they didn't know any better. You can bet that they had all kinds of judgments about themselves, and that everybody else was judging them, too. They lived in the dream of the first attention, *the underworld*, the dream that we call *Hades*, or *hell*. They were dead.

Of course, all these symbols are not exactly the truth. The truth is *behind* the symbols — it's in the *intent* or the *meaning* of the symbols. When religions describe the dream of hell, they say it's a place where we burn, a place where we are judged, a place of eternal punishment. Well, that description of hell is the ordinary dream of the humans. That very same thing is happening in the human mind — the judgment, the guilt, the punishment, and the emotions generated by fear that feel like a fire burning inside us. Fear is king of the underworld, and it rules our world by creating the distortions in our knowledge. Fear creates the whole world of injustice and emotional drama, the whole nightmare that billions of people are living in.

And what is the biggest fear in this world? Fear of the truth. Humans are afraid of the truth because we have learned to believe so many lies. Of course, we're also afraid of the lies we believe. Truth or fiction, just having knowledge makes us feel safe, but then we suffer because we believe what we know, and almost everything we know isn't true. It's just a point of view, but we believe it, and we deliver the same distorted messages to our own children. The whole chain continues, and the history of the humans repeats itself again, and again, and again.

Long ago, wise people compared the dream of the first attention to a marketplace where thousands of people are talking at the same time and nobody is really listening. The Toltec call this a *mitote*, which is a Náhuatl word meaning "extreme gossip." In that *mitote*, we use the word against ourselves, and when we relate with other people we use the word against them.

Every human is a magician, and in the interaction between the magicians, there are spells being cast everywhere. How? By misusing the word, by taking everything personally, by distorting everything we perceive with assumptions, by gossiping and spreading emotional poison with the word. Humans cast spells mainly upon the people we love the most, and the more authority we have, the more powerful the spells. Authority is the power that a human has to control other humans, to make them obey. You can see yourself as a child being afraid of authority. You can also see adults being afraid of authority. Words spoken with authority become a powerful spell that affects other humans. Why? Because we *believe* those words.

If we understand the power of symbology, we can see where the symbols are taking us. We can see it by the way we behave, by the interaction we have with everybody, but mainly with ourselves. We become possessed by an idea, by a belief, by a story. Sometimes it's anger that possesses us; sometimes it's jealousy that possesses us; sometimes it's love that possesses us. The symbols are competing for control of our attention, and in one way or another they're changing all the time; they're taking turns possessing us. There are thousands of symbols that want to take their place in our head and control us. As we said before, all those symbols are alive, and that life comes from us because we *believe.*

The symbols are talking and talking inside our head. They never stop. It's just as if we have a narrator in our head telling us everything that is happening around us, as if we are not aware that we are perceiving it. "And now the sun is going down. That's good. I'm hot. Look, there are trees over there! What is that person doing? I wonder what he's thinking." The voice of knowledge wants to know what everything means. It can hardly wait to interpret everything that happens in our lives. It's telling us what to do, when to do it, where to do it, how to do it. It's reminding us all the time what we believe about ourselves, what we don't believe about ourselves. It's telling us everything that we are not. It's asking us why we can't be the way we should be.

In the dream of the first attention, the world we live in is just like a reality show, hosted by the voice of knowledge. And for sure we are always going to be right and everyone else is going to be wrong because we use everything that we know to justify everything in our show. What a reality show! Rated number one. We create every character in that story, and whatever we believe about every one of them is not the truth, and it never was the truth. With a whole Tree of Knowledge living in our head, we no longer perceive the truth — we only perceive our own knowledge; we only perceive lies. When we only perceive lies, our attention becomes trapped in the dream of hell; we no longer perceive the reality of heaven all around us. And this is how humans fell from Paradise.

In the story of Adam and Eve, we had a great exchange with a snake who lived in the Tree of Knowledge. That snake was a fallen angel who delivered distorted messages; he was the Prince of Lies, and we were innocent. The snake said to us, "Do you want to be like God?" A simple question, but can you see the trick? If we had said, "No, thank you, I am already God," we would still be living in Paradise, but we answered, "Yes, I want to be like God." We didn't notice the lie; we bit the fruit, we swallowed the lie, and we died.

What makes us bite the apple without noticing the lie is the doubt. Before we have the doubt, we don't even know; the truth is there, and we just live it. Once we ingest the lie, we no longer believe that we are God, and this is when we start to search for God. Next we believe that we have to create a temple to find God; we need a place to worship God. We have to sacrifice everything to reach God; we have to create pain in ourselves, and offer our pain to God. Very soon we have a big temple with thousands of people believing that they are not God. Of course, we need to give God a name, and the result is the creation of religion.

We create the god of thunder, the god of war, the goddess of love, and we call them Zeus, Mars, and Aphrodite. There were thousands, maybe millions, of people who believed in these gods, and worshiped these gods. They offered their lives as a sacrifice to these gods. They even killed their own children as an offering to these gods because they believed these gods were the truth. But were they?

As you can see, the first lie that we believe is "I am not God." From this lie comes another lie, and then another, and then another, and we believe and believe and believe. Very soon there are so many lies that it's overwhelming, and we forget our own divinity. We see the beauty and perfection of God, and we want to be like God — we want to be that "image of perfection" — and we search and search for perfection.

Humans are storytellers, and we tell our children stories about a god who is perfect, about a god who judges us and punishes us when we misbehave. We tell them about a Santa Claus who rewards little children who are "good," or more like "God." These messages are distorted. The kind of god who plays with justice doesn't exist. Santa Claus doesn't exist. All that knowledge in our head isn't real.

You see, when we talk to the snake in the Tree of Knowledge, we talk to a distorted reflection of ourselves. That snake in the Tree of Knowledge is who we are really so afraid of. We're afraid of our own reflection. Isn't that silly? Imagine looking at a reflection of yourself in the mirror. The reflection appears to be an exact copy of what is real, but the image in the mirror is the opposite of what is real; your right hand is your left hand in the mirror. The truth is always distorted by the reflection.

When we are children, the mirrors around us hook our attention so we can see them, and what we see are distorted images of ourselves, according to their mood, according to the moment when those mirrors are reflecting to us, according to whatever belief system they are using to justify their perceptions. The humans around us tell us what they *believe* we are, but there isn't a clear mirror to reflect what we *really* are. All the mirrors are completely distorted. They project what they believe onto us, and almost everything they believe is a lie. We believe it or we don't believe it, but when we are children, we are innocent and we believe almost everything. We put our faith in lies; we give them life, we give them power, and soon those lies are ruling our lives.

The story of the Prince of Lies is just a story, but it's a beautiful story made with symbols that we can understand and then draw conclusions. I think its meaning is clear. Once we start dreaming that we are not God, the whole nightmare begins. We fall from Paradise and go directly to the underworld, to what we call *hell*. We begin to search for God, we begin to search for our *self*, because the Tree of Knowledge is living our life and our authentic self is dead.

And this reminds me of another story about Jesus the Christ, who was walking with his disciples when he saw a man who was worthy of his teachings. He went to the man and said, "Come and join me." The man replied, "I will come, but my father just died. I have to bury him, and then I will follow you." And Jesus told him, "Let the dead bury the dead. You are alive. Come with me."

If you understand the story, it's easy to see that you are "dead" when you are not awake, when you are not aware of what you are. You are *truth*; you are *life*; you are *love*. But in the process of domestication, the outside dream, the dream of the planet, hooks your attention, and feeds you all of your beliefs. Little by little, you become a copy of the outside dream. You copy everything you learn from everybody and everything around you. You copy not just beliefs but behavior, which means you copy not just what people say but what they do. You perceive the emotional state of the people around you, and you even copy that.

You are not who you *really* are, because you have been possessed by that distorted image of you. And this may be a little difficult to understand, but all this time it has been you who possesses *you*. What is possessing you is the *virtual* you. It's what you *think* you are; it's what you *believe* you are, and that image of yourself becomes extremely powerful. All these years of practice have made you a master of pretending to be what you think you are. And that distorted image of yourself is really your grave, because the real you is not the one who is living your life. And who is living your life?

Is it the real you who creates all the drama and suffering in your life? Is it the real you who says "Life is a valley of tears, and we come here to suffer?" Is it the real you who judges yourself and punishes yourself, and invites other people to punish you, too? Is it the real you who abuses your body? Is it the real you who doesn't even like yourself? Is it *really* the real you who's dreaming all that?

No, it's not the real you. You are dead, and that's the truth. And what is the key to coming back to life? *Awareness*. When you recover awareness, you resurrect and come back to life. In the Christian tradition, the resurrection day is when the Christ comes back from the dead and shows his divinity to the world. That's why you are here: to come back from the dead and reclaim your own divinity. It's time to come back from the world of illusion, the world of lies, and return to your own truth, to your own authenticity. It's time to unlearn the lies and become the real you. And in order to do that, you need to come back to life, which is truth.

Awareness is the key to coming back to life, and it's one of the main masteries of the Toltec. Awareness takes you out of the dream of the first attention, into the dream of the second attention, where you rebel against all the lies that are ruling your head. You rebel, and the whole dream starts changing.

10

THE DREAM OF THE SECOND ATTENTION

The Warriors

THE FIRST TIME THAT WE LEARN HOW TO DREAM, there are many things that we don't like, that we are against, but we just accept the dream as it is. Then, for whatever reason, we become aware that we don't like the way we are living our lives; we become aware of what we are dreaming, and we don't want that dream. Now we try to use the attention a second time to change our dream, to create a second dream. This is what the Toltec call *the dream of the second attention*, or *the dream of the warriors*, because now we declare a war against all the lies in our knowledge.

In the dream of the second attention, we begin to doubt: "Maybe everything I learned is not the truth." We begin to challenge what we believe; we start to question all the opinions that we learned. We know there is something in our head that makes us do many things that perhaps we don't want to do — something that has complete control of our mind — and we don't like it. And because we don't like it, at a certain point we begin to rebel.

In that rebellion, we try to recover our authenticity, what I call the *integrity* of the self, or the totality of what we are. In the dream of the first attention, the authentic self has no chance; it's a complete victim. We don't rebel; we don't even try. But now we no longer want to be the victim, and we try to change our world. We try to recover our personal freedom — the freedom to be who we really are, the freedom to do what we really want to do. The world of the warriors is the world of trying. We try to change the world that we don't like, and we keep trying, and trying, and trying, and the war looks endless.

In the dream of the warriors, we are in a war, but that war is not against other people. It has nothing to do with the outside dream. The whole thing is happening inside our mind. It's a war against the part of our mind that makes all the choices that guide us into our personal hell. It's a war between the authentic self and what we call *the tyrant, the big judge, the book of law, the belief system*. It's a war between ideas, between opinions, between beliefs. I also call it *the war of the gods* because all these ideas fight for dominion of the human mind. And just like the gods of antiquity, they claim a human sacrifice.

Yes, the human sacrifice we offer to the gods is still happening, even if we claim that we don't believe in human sacrifice anymore. Of course, we change the names of the gods; we change the *meaning* of all those symbols that we call *god*. Perhaps we no longer believe in Apollo, we no longer believe in Zeus, we no longer believe in Osiris; but we believe in justice, we believe in liberty, we believe in democracy. These are the names of the new gods. We give our power to these symbols, we take them to the realm of the gods, and we sacrifice our lives in the name of these gods.

Human sacrifice is happening all the time, all around the world, and we can see the result: We see violence, we see crime, we see jails full of people, we see war, we see the dream of hell in humanity because we believe in so many superstitions and distortions in our knowledge. Humans create wars, and we send our young to be sacrificed in those wars. Many times they don't even know what they are fighting for.

We see a war of gangs in any large city. Young people sacrifice themselves and kill one another in the name of pride, in the name of profit, in the name of whatever god they believe in. They fight for their pride, they fight for control of a piece of land, they fight for a symbol that's in their heads and on their jackets, and they sacrifice themselves. From the smallest barrio to the largest nations around the planet, we see groups of people fighting and defending their gods for something that doesn't exist. The war is raging inside their heads, but the problem is that they send the war outside of themselves and kill one another.

Perhaps we no longer believe in human sacrifice, but right now there are people who say, "I will be the one who sacrifices. Give me a gun, and I will kill as many people as I can before they kill me." And this is not a judgment; it's just the way it is. I will not say that human sacrifice is wrong. It just exists, and we cannot deny that it exists because we see it every day in many different cultures around the world. We see it, and we also participate in it. If someone makes a mistake and is caught breaking a rule, what do we do? Let's crucify him, let's judge him, let's gossip about him. That's another form of human sacrifice. Yes, there are rules, and maybe it's the biggest sin to go against those rules, and maybe some of those rules are completely unnatural. But we create the rules, we agree to live by those rules, and we will follow those rules until we no longer need them, and right now we need them.

Humans believe in so many lies that even the smallest thing becomes a big demon that makes us suffer. Usually it's just a judgment, and mainly it's a self-judgment: "Poor me. Look what happened to me when I was nine years old. Look what happened to me last night!" Well, whatever happened in your past is not truth anymore. It could be the most horrible thing, but right now it's not truth, because right now is the only truth you live in. Whatever happened in your past is in the virtual reality, and whatever happened to your body was healed long ago, but the mind can make you suffer and live in shame for years.

Humans carry our past, our history, around with us, and it's just like we're carrying a heavy corpse.

For some it's not that heavy, but for the majority of people that corpse is very heavy. And it's not just heavy; it smells very bad. What many of us do is keep our corpse to share with the ones we love. With the powerful memory we have, we bring it to life in the present moment and relive our experiences again, and again, and again. Every time we remember those experiences, we punish ourselves and everybody else again, and again, and again.

Humans are the only animals on earth who punish themselves a thousand times or more for the same mistake, and who punish everybody else a thousand times or more for the same mistake. How can we talk about injustice in the rest of the world when there is no justice in the world inside our own head? The entire universe is ruled by justice, but by true justice, not by the distortion of justice that we artists have created. True justice is facing what I call *action-reaction*. We live in a world of consequences; for every action there's a reaction. True justice is to pay one time for every mistake we make. And how many times do we pay for every mistake? Obviously, this is not justice.

Let's say that you're living with guilt and shame for a mistake that you made ten years ago. The excuse for your suffering is "I made a terrible mistake," and you think you're still suffering for something that happened ten years ago, but the truth is that you're suffering from something that happened ten seconds ago. You judged yourself again for the same mistake, and of course the big judge says, "You need to be punished." It's simple action-reaction. The *action* is self-judgment; the *reaction* is self-punishment in the form of guilt and shame. All your life you repeat the same action, hoping to have a different reaction, and it never happens. The only way to change your life is to change the action, and then the reaction will change.

Can you see how you, knowledge, are hurting you, the human? You're thinking and judging with all those symbols that you learned. You're creating a story that's abusing the human. Whenever the human is abused, the normal reaction is anger, hate, jealousy, or any of the emotions that make us suffer. Our nervous system is a factory of emotions, and the emotions we experience depend on what we perceive. Well, we perceive our own judgments, our own belief system, our own voice of knowledge. And with the judge, the victim, and the belief system ruling our virtual world, the emotions we generate are fear, anger, jealousy, guilt, shame. What else can we expect to create? Love? Of course not, though sometimes we do.

The word is a force you cannot see, but you can see the manifestation of that force, the expression of the word, which is your own life. The way to measure the impeccability of your word is by your emotional reaction. Are you happy or are you suffering? If you're enjoying your dream or suffering your dream, it's because you're creating it that way. Yes, your parents, your religion, the schools, the government, the entire society helped you to create your dream, and it's true that you never had a choice.

But now you have a choice. You can create heaven, or you can create hell. Remember, both are states of mind that exist within you.

Do you like to be happy? Then be happy and enjoy your happiness. Do you like to suffer? Great; then why not enjoy your suffering? If you choose to create hell, good for you. Cry, have pain, make a masterpiece of art with your pain. But if you have awareness, there is no way you are going to choose hell; you are going to choose heaven. And the way to choose heaven is by being impeccable with your word.

If you're impeccable with your word, how can you judge yourself? How can you blame yourself? How can you carry guilt or shame? When you are not creating all those emotions, you feel wonderful! Now you smile again, and it's completely authentic. You don't have to pretend to be a certain way. You don't try to be what you are not. Whatever you are is what you will be in that moment. In that moment, you accept yourself just the way you are.

You like yourself; you enjoy being with yourself. You no longer abuse yourself by using the symbols against yourself.

That's why I have to repeat that it's so important to be aware. The tyranny of the symbols is extremely powerful. In the dream of the second attention, the warrior tries to find out how the symbols took power over the human. The whole war of the warrior is against the symbols, against our own creation, and it's not because we hate the symbols. The symbols are a masterful creation; they're our art, and it's convenient for us to use all those symbols to communicate. But when we give all our power to those symbols, we become powerless, and we need to be rescued. We need a savior because we don't have the power to make it on our own.

Then we look outside ourselves and say, "Oh God, please save me." But it's not up to God or Jesus or Buddha or Moses or Muhammed or any master, shaman, or guru to save us. We can't blame them if they don't save us. Nobody can save us, because nobody else is responsible for whatever happens in our virtual world. The priest, the minister, the rabbi, the shaman, or the guru cannot change our world; our husband or our wife, our children, or our friends cannot change it. No one else can change our world, because that world only lives in our head.

Many people say that Jesus died for us, to save us from our sins. Well, it's a wonderful story, but Jesus doesn't make the choices in our lives. Instead of saving us, Jesus told us what to do. You need help? Okay, you need to follow the truth. You need to forgive. Love one another. He gave us all the tools, but we say, "No. I cannot forgive. I prefer to live with my emotional poison, with my pride, with my anger and my jealousy." If we are fighting with the people we love, if we're creating a lot of resistance around us, remember, we live in a world of consequences. We have to let go of that first, we have to forgive, because forgiveness is the only way to clear our emotional body of emotional poison.

All of us have emotional poison because all of us have emotional wounds. It happens. Just as it's normal for our body to hurt when we have a cut, or when we fall and break a bone, it's normal for the emotional body to hurt because we are alive, because we are surrounded by predators, and we are predators also. But there's no one to blame; it's just the way it is. If we blame, it's our emotional poison that makes us blame. Instead of blaming, we can take responsibility for our own healing.

If you're waiting for someone to come and save you, well, you have to save yourself. You are your own savior, but there are teachers who give you tools to help you recover awareness and win your personal war. There are artists who can show you how to create a masterpiece of heaven with your art.

Let's say that you're a good artist, but then a master artist comes along and says, "I like you. I want you to be my apprentice. Come; I will teach you. The first and most important tool for you to become a master artist is *be impeccable with your word.*

It's something so simple. You write your own story, and you don't want to write the story against yourself. Second, *don't take anything personally.* That will help you a lot; most of the drama goes away if you just agree with that. Third, *don't make assumptions.* Don't create your own hell; stop believing in superstitions and lies. And fourth, *always do your best.* Take action. Practice makes the master. Very simple."

Then the moment comes when you start to see your whole creation from another point of view. You start to realize that you are the artistic creator of your life. You are the one who creates the canvas, the paint, the paintbrush, and the art. You are the one who gives meaning to every stroke on the canvas of your life. You are the one who invests all your faith in your art. And you say, "The story I'm creating is beautiful, but I don't believe it anymore. I don't believe my story or anybody else's story. I can see that it's just art." Great. That's the fifth agreement. Come back to common sense, to the truth, to the *real* you. *Be skeptical, but learn to listen.*

In the dream of the second attention, you need tools to win the war and change your world, and that's what these agreements are all about. These are the tools for transforming your dream, for mastering your dream, and it's up to you what you do with these tools. These five simple agreements have the power to plant a seed of doubt in all those limiting, fear-based agreements you made your whole life. The only chance you have to unlearn the lies in your knowledge is by use of the attention. You use the attention to put your first dream together, and you use the attention to unlearn that dream.

The Four Agreements are the tools for using your attention a second time to create your personal heaven, and the fifth agreement is the tool to win the war against the tyranny of the symbols. The Four Agreements are tools for your personal transformation, and the fifth agreement is the end of personal transformation and the beginning of giving yourself the greatest gift that you can give yourself: the gift of *doubt*.

We have said that it was doubt that made us fall out of Paradise. Well, coming back to Paradise is once again about doubt. Doubt is the tool we use to recover our faith, to take our power back from every lie and superstition we believe in, and return that power to ourselves. Of course, we can also use the power of doubt against ourselves by doubting ourselves, by doubting the truth. In the story of Adam and Eve, when we doubt that we are God, that doubt opens the door to another doubt, and then another, and another. When we doubt the truth, we start to believe in lies. Soon we believe in so many lies that we no longer see the truth, and we fall from the dream of heaven.

Doubt is a great creation we made for going into hell or getting out of hell. Either way, doubt opens the door to be possessed by symbols, or doubt closes the door to stop the possession. If we doubt ourselves, if we doubt the truth, the whole Tree of Knowledge — all the mythology that controlled our attention our entire lives — starts coming back to us.

The voice of knowledge starts possessing us again, and we begin to feel the anger, the jealousy, the injustice that come with all the symbols, with all the assumptions, with all that *thinking*.

Then instead of doubting yourself, have faith in yourself. Instead of doubting the truth, doubt the lies. *Be skeptical, but learn to listen.* The fifth agreement opens the door to heaven, and the rest is up to you. This agreement is about being in heaven and heaven being in you. It's about letting go of your attachment to symbols, even your own name, and merging with the infinite — to become authentic, to believe in yourself without a doubt, because even a little doubt can end the experience of heaven.

When you have faith in yourself, you follow every instinct that you were born with. You have no doubt about what you are, and you return to common sense. You have all the power of your authenticity; you trust yourself, you trust *life*. You trust that everything is going to be just fine, and life becomes extremely easy. The mind no longer needs to understand everything; it doesn't need to *know*. You know something or you don't know it, but you don't have any doubt if you know or not. If you don't know, you accept that you don't know. You're not going to make it up. When you are completely authentic, you speak the truth to yourself, without any doubt: "I like it; I don't like it. I want it; I don't want it." You don't have to do what you don't like to do. You enjoy your life doing exactly what you like to do.

We make life difficult when we try to sacrifice ourselves for somebody else. Surely, you are not here to sacrifice yourself for anybody. You are not here to satisfy other people's opinions or points of view. In *the dream of the second attention*, one of the first challenges is the fear of being yourself — your *real* self. If you have the courage to face this challenge, you find out that all the reasons you were afraid don't even exist. Then you find out that it's much easier to be yourself than to try to be what you are not. The whole dream of hell makes you tired because it takes energy to uphold an image, to wear a social mask. You're tired of faking it; you're tired of not being *you.* Just being authentic is the best thing you can do. When you're authentic, you can do whatever you want to do; you can believe whatever you want to believe, and that includes believing in yourself.

How difficult can it be to have faith in yourself, to believe in *you* instead of believing in symbols? You can put your faith in scientific theories, in so many religions, opinions, and points of view, but this is not *real* faith. Faith in yourself is the real faith. Real faith is to trust yourself unconditionally, because you know what you really are, and what you really are is the truth.

Once you recover awareness of what you are, the war in your head is over. It's obvious that you are the one who creates all the symbols. And because it's obvious where the power of your word comes from, your word has power, and nothing can stop the power of your word. Your word becomes impeccable, and it's impeccable because you have power over the symbols instead of the symbols having power over you. Once your word is impeccable, you base every choice of your life on the truth, and you win the war against the tyrant. The words are there, ready to be used at your command, but the words only have meaning when you use them to communicate, to have a direct connection with someone. After you stop using the words, they have no meaning again.

By the end of the dream of the second attention, the human form starts to break apart, and your reality changes once again. It changes because you no longer perceive the world through a rigid structure of beliefs. The war is over because your faith is not invested in lies. Even though lies still exist, you no longer *believe*. As you know, the truth just is; you don't have to believe the truth. You don't believe anything anymore, but you can see, and what you can see is the truth. The truth is right here; it's unique, and it's perfect. Maybe not the way you interpret it, maybe not the way you use the word to gossip about yourself or to gossip about other people, but once you see the truth, who cares what other people are dreaming? It's not important what other people around you are dreaming. What's important is your own experience — to use all the tools you have to face what you believe, to see the truth, to win your personal war.

You don't need to compete with anybody; you don't need to compare yourself with anybody. You just need to be what you are, to be love, but *real* love, not the kind of love that possesses you and makes you believe in love. Not the love that makes you become jealous and possessive of others, and puts you directly in hell with all the tortures and punishments of hell. Not the love that makes you sacrifice in the name of love, or makes you hurt yourself and hurt others in the name of love. The symbol of love has become so distorted. Real love is what you were born with. Real love is what you are.

You were born with everything you need to make it. If you face your fears today, tomorrow you will see the dream of the second attention, the world of the warriors. But just because you win against fear today, it doesn't mean that you have won the war. No, the war isn't over; the war has just begun. You are still judging; you still have all those issues. You think it's done, and boom! Your tyrant is back. Oh yes, again, and again, and again. And it's not just the tyrant in you; it's the tyrant in everybody around you, and there are some that are worse than others. But even if you have been at war for many years, at least you can defend yourself. As a warrior, you may win the war or you may lose the war, but once you have awareness, you are no longer a victim; you are at war, and that's where the majority of people are right now, until the war is over.

In the dream of the second attention, you begin to create your personal heaven on earth. You begin to put your faith in agreements that support *life*, that add to your joy, to your happiness, to your freedom. But this is just one step of your evolution. There's much more than that. The moment is coming when you master awareness, which means you master the truth. And by the way, you also master transformation; you master love, intent, or faith, because by that time, you believe in yourself.

The result of this transformation is the creation of another reality that has the same frame as the first two dreams, but in this other reality you no longer believe what you used to believe. You no longer believe the lies that you learned; you don't even believe the words that you learned. You have no doubt about what you experience, about what you are.

The next dream, the dream of the third attention, is not that far away. But first you have to win the war in your head, and now you have the tools to do it. Then why not do it? Take the action, but don't *try* anymore. If you try, you will die trying, and I can assure you that millions of warriors have died trying. There are very few warriors who ever win the war that's happening in the human mind, but those who win the war by using their attention a second time re-create their entire world.

11

THE DREAM OF THE THIRD ATTENTION

The Masters

THE DREAM OF THE SECOND ATTENTION ENDS when something very important happens in our lives, something called *the last judgment*. This is the very last time we judge either ourselves or anybody else. It's the day we accept ourselves just the way we are, and we accept everybody else just the way they are. When the day of our last judgment comes, the war in our head is over, and *the dream of the third attention* begins. And it will be the end of our world, but also the beginning of our world, because we are no longer in the dream of the warriors. We are in the upper world, or what I call *the dream of the masters.*

The masters are former warriors. They have won their personal war, and they are at peace. *The dream of the masters* is a dream of truth, a dream of respect, a dream full of love and joy. It's the playground of life; it's what we are meant to live, and only awareness can take us to that place.

Many religions talk about the last judgment as if it's a punishment for sinners. They describe it as the day when God comes and judges us, and destroys all the sinners. This isn't true. The last judgment is a card in the Tarot, which is an ancient mythology from Egypt. When the mystery schools talk about the last judgment, we can hardly wait for that day because it's the day when the dead come out of their grave, which means we resurrect. It's the day when we recover awareness, and awaken from the dream of the underworld. It's the day when we're no longer afraid to be alive again. This is when we come back to our real state, our divine self, where we feel a communion of love with everything in existence.

The resurrection is a wonderful concept from mystery schools all around the world. Once you have the awareness that almost everything you learned through symbols is not the truth, the only thing left is just to enjoy life, and that's the resurrection. When you give meaning to everything through symbols, your attention is dispersed on many things at once. When you take away the meaning from everything, you are in communion, and you become the whole thing to yourself. You become the only living being that exists. There's no difference between you and any star in the sky, or you and any rock in the desert. Everything in existence is part of the only living being in existence. When you experience this truth, even for a moment, the whole structure of your belief system disappears, and you are in that wonderful dream of heaven.

Today can be a day just like every other day, or today can be a day of celebration, the day of your resurrection, the day that you change your world by coming back to life. It can be the day for the real you to come out of that grave of believing that you are what you *think* you are, and become what you *really* are.

In the dream of the third attention, you finally have the awareness of what you are, but not with words. And because there are no words to explain what you are, you go back into peace, the place where you don't need to use words to know what you are. This is what the masters in the esoteric philosophies would reveal to their apprentices. The highest point you can reach is when you go beyond symbols and become one with life, with God.

Ancient religions claim that nobody can say the name of God, and it's absolutely true, because there is no symbol to describe God. The only way to know God is to be God. When you become God, you say, "Oh, that's why I could not learn the symbol."

The truth is that we don't know the name of the one who created us. The word *God* is just a symbol that represents what *really* exists, and I resist this word because it's a symbol that has become so distorted. If we use symbols to describe God, we need to agree on the meaning of the symbols, and then what point of view are we using? There are billions of different points of view. As an artist, I do my best to paint God with words, and it's the only thing I can offer — a picture of God from my personal point of view. Whatever I say, of course, is just a story that's only the truth for me. And maybe this will make sense to you, and maybe it won't, but at least you will have an idea of my personal point of view.

The dream of the masters is a little difficult to explain because the real teaching is not with words. It's with the presence. If you could feel the presence of a master, you would learn much more than you can from words. Words can't express even a tiny bit of the experience, but if you use your imagination, words can take you to the place where you can have the experience for yourself. And this is my intention right now — for you to expand your awareness to the point where you can *perceive* what you really are, where you can *feel* what you really are.

Instead of using words, perhaps a better way is to put you face to face with God, so you can see God. And if I show you God, face to face, what you are going to see is yourself. Believe it or don't believe it, but you will see yourself because you are the manifestation of God. And if you could see what's *moving* your body, then you would see the *real* God. Look at your own hand. Move your fingers. The force that moves your fingers is what the Toltec call *intent*, or what I call *life, the infinite*, or *God*.

Intent is the only living being that exists, and it's that force that is moving everything. You are not the fingers. You are the force that is moving them. The fingers obey you. You can give whatever explanation you want: "Oh, my brain, my nerves. . . ." But if you go for the truth, the force that moves your fingers is the same force that makes you dream; it's the same force that opens a flower, or moves the wind, or creates a tornado, or makes the stars move throughout the universe, or makes electrons move around atoms. There is only one living being, and *you* are that being. You are that force that manifests itself in infinite ways throughout all the universes.

The first manifestation of that force is light, or energy, which is the same thing, and everything is created through this energy. Scientists know that everything is made of energy, and since there is only one force in the universe that creates this energy, at this point science and religion come together, and we can understand that we are God because we are light. That is what we are; that is what everything is, in billions and billions of different frequencies or manifestations of light. And together, all the different frequencies create only one light.

Intent is the force that creates the light, and we can say that light is the messenger of intent, because it carries the message of life that goes everywhere. Light has all the information to create everything in existence, including any kind of life — humans, monkeys, dogs, trees — anything. All species of life on planet Earth are created from a specific ray or frequency of light that scientists call DNA. And the difference between the DNA itself may be minimal, but in the manifestation it could be the difference between a human and a monkey, or a human and a jaguar, or a human and a tree.

Light has many properties. It's alive. It's a living being, and it's extremely intelligent. It's creating all of the time; it's transforming all of the time, and it cannot be destroyed. Light is everywhere and everything is full of light, but we cannot see light unless it's reflected by matter. If we send an object into space from planet Earth, we see the object because it is reflecting light. There are no empty spaces between the stars, between the galaxies, between all the universes, which means all the universes are connected.

You are a whole universe. The earth is another universe. The sun and all the planets around the sun are another universe. All the solar systems together create another universe, and we can keep going and going, until we see only one living being made by billions and billions of different living beings.

Every living being is protected by the force that we call *soul*. The soul is the force that puts an entire universe together and recognizes the totality of that being. The soul makes matter impenetrable, which means it creates what looks like a division between beings. The soul gives shape to everything; without this force, there would be no difference between you and a flower or a fish or a bird. Your soul was born at the moment of your conception, and it recognizes every element of itself — every molecule, every cell, every organ of your being. Your soul recognizes everything that belongs to your universe, and it rejects everything that doesn't belong to it.

In the dream of the third attention, you're aware that your body is a whole universe made by billions of living beings — made by atoms, made by molecules, made by cells, made by tissues, made by organs, made by systems, until the whole universe is one.

And from the point of view of the mind, it looks like there's only one point of view — the one behind your eyes. But if you go deep into awareness, you find that every atom in your body has a personal point of view because every atom is alive. Every atom is an entire universe; it's nothing but a miniature solar system with stars and planets. What every universe has in common is that each one of them is alive with the total power of the infinite.

You, that force, are alive; you are total power. You are truth; you are real. Everything else, including everything you know through symbols, is not truth. It's not real. It's an illusion, and it's beautiful. Light is not just intelligent; it has memory. It creates an image of itself; it creates the whole world of illusion that becomes your mind, the way you dream. Your dreams are not matter; they are a reflection of matter, and that reflection exists in the matter that we call the *brain*. The brain is nothing but a mirror. As we said before, if you look inside a mirror, you are seeing your own mind, your own dream.

The first time you open your eyes, you start to perceive light, and light becomes your teacher. Light projects information into your eyes that you don't understand, but you were made to perceive light, to become one with light, because light is your other half. And because you are light, you are always creating, and always transforming, and always evolving. Light goes directly into your brain, and rearranges your brain in order to modify you, virtual reality, to make you a better reflection of itself. When light is modifying your brain, the brain by itself is modifying God's factory, the DNA, for the next possible human being that can come from you.

And just as your body has many different organs — brain, heart, lungs, liver, stomach, skin— that all together create *you*, a totality, every organ in your body is made by different kinds of cells that create that organ. Do the cells know that together all of the cells are only one living being, which means *you*? Do we humans know that together all of the humans are only one living being, which means *humanity*?

You are surrounded by billions of humans. Just like you, they were programmed to be human. Male or female, you recognize them; you know they are humans, like you. You *know*. But perhaps what you don't know is that we humans are an organ of the beautiful planet Earth. Planet Earth is alive. It's a living being, and the entire humanity works for the planet as an organ of that living being. The forests are another organ, the atmosphere is another organ — every species is another organ — and we all work together to create an equilibrium that is the metabolism of planet Earth.

All of humanity is only one living being, and this is no longer a theory. We humans live together. We have the same kind of body; we have the same kind of mind; we have the same needs. We create all those symbols to understand one another. Male or female, victims, warriors, or masters, we are all the same. No human is better or worse than any other human. No human is better or worse than anything that exists throughout the universe. At the deepest level of our being, there is no difference between a human and a dog, or a human and a flea, or a fly, or a flower. We are the same; we come from the same place, and it doesn't matter where our story comes from. It doesn't matter if we are a Christian, a Buddhist, a Muslim, a Hindu. We come from the same place, and we're going back to the same place.

The infinite creates everything in existence, and when the cycle is over, everything returns to the infinite. Of course the body dies, because the body is mortal, but *you*, the force, are immortal. In that force where the mind lives, the only thing that dies are the lies. In ancient Egypt, it was said: If your heart is lighter than a feather when you die, then welcome to heaven. If your heart is heavier than a feather, you are not going to heaven. Lies cannot go back into power, but the truth returns to power, because the truth is the reflection of power; it's the reflection of the infinite. The question becomes: How heavy are your lies? Is your heart burdened with anger, fear, guilt, regret?

In the dream of the third attention, the truth has already destroyed all the lies, and the only thing that survives is the truth, which means the real you. You are that force. You are life, which is truth, and from that point your dream becomes heaven. Your dream becomes a beautiful masterpiece of art, a beautiful masterpiece of love. This leads you to the third mastery of the Toltec, *the mastery of love*, or we can also call it *the mastery of intent*, or *faith*. I prefer to call it *the mastery of faith* because it's a mastery for you to trust in yourself, which means realizing the power that you have: the power of intent, the power of life, the power of belief, the power of faith, the power of love. They're all the same power, of course. They're *total power*.

In the moment when you master faith, you live your life in love, because love is what you are, and it's wonderful. In that moment, you completely accept your body, your emotions, your life, your story. You respect yourself; you respect all of the artists, all of your brothers and sisters; you respect all of creation.

You love yourself unconditionally, and you are not afraid to express your love, to say "I love you" to others. When you master faith, when you live your life in love, you see your own love being reflected in every secondary character of your story, and you love every secondary character of your story unconditionally, just as you love yourself.

This changes your relationship with the rest of the humans. It makes you completely impersonal. You don't need reasons to love someone or not to love someone; you don't even *choose* to love, because to love is your nature. Love is coming out of you like the light from the sun. All of your nature is coming out of you, just as it is, without expectations. And your love has nothing to do with words in your head. There are no stories. It's an experience that we call *communion*, which means to have the same frequency, the same vibration, as love. This is how you used to be before you learned to speak, because you have evolved from the whole deep hell of the dream of the first attention into a better dream, the dream of the second attention, until you dream the dream of the third attention, where you know that everything you are seeing, everything you are dreaming, is a virtual reality made by light.

For thousands of years, people have known that there are three worlds that exist within every human. In almost every philosophy and mythology, we find that people have divided everything into three worlds, but they have called them by different names and have used different symbols to describe them. As we have seen in the artist's tradition, which means the Toltec, these three worlds are known as *the dream of the first attention, the dream of the second attention,* and *the dream of the third attention.* In Greece and Egypt, they were known as *the underworld, the world,* and *the upper world.* In the Christian tradition, they are known as *hell, purgatory,* and *paradise.*

The concept of the world that we have today is in many ways different than what people understood thousands of years ago. For them, the world was not the planet; the world was everything that we can perceive, everything that we know. That is why it was said that every head is a world, because each of us creates an entire world in our head, and we live in that world. The majority of humans live in the dream of the first attention, the underworld. Another large part of humanity lives in the dream of the second attention, the world of the warriors, and it's because of this dream that humanity is going in the right direction and evolving the way it is.

We usually believe that the upper world is all about goodness and the underworld is all about fear and evil, but that's not exactly true. All three worlds exist within every human. We carry the underworld within us, just as we carry the upper world within us. In the underworld, a whole infinity exists, and in the upper world, there also exists a whole infinity, and both meet in the world, which is where we live. The way to the underworld becomes a choice, just as the way to the upper world becomes a choice.

In the dream of the masters, we are aware that to make a choice is to have a power in our hands.

We control our whole dream by making choices. Every choice has consequences, and a dream master is aware of the consequences. Making a choice can open many doors, and close many other doors. Not making a choice is also a choice that we can make. By making choices, we can master the art of dreaming and create the most beautiful life.

Anybody can be a great dream artist, but the mastery comes when we have complete control over our dream, which means we recover control of our own attention. When we master the attention, we really master intent, which means we have complete control over our choices. The dream of our life is going to go wherever we want to take it.

In the ordinary dream of the humans, the belief system controls the attention. And because our personal power, our will, is weak, anyone can hook our attention and insert an opinion in our mind. The will, or intent, is the force that can move what exists, or change the direction of what exists. The will is what holds the attention and moves the attention.

Once we have enough power that we can use our will, we gain control of the attention. Then we can finally gain control of our beliefs and win the war for the control of our dream.

In the dream of the third attention, we are not putting our attention on life. We *are* life, we *are* the force, we *are* intent, and intent controls the attention. The dream of the third attention is the dream of pure intent. We become aware that we are life — not just as a concept, but as an action, as complete awareness. Now we can see with the eyes of truth, and this is a completely different point of view.

The first time you learn how to dream, your belief system creates millions of little barriers to the truth. When the structure of your belief system is no longer there, you take away the barriers, and you no longer see only one point of view. There are many points of view that you can see at the same time. You see yourself not just from the point of view of a human, but from the point of view of a force. You see yourself not just as a force, but as the manifestation of that force. You know that you are light, that you are just an image in the light, and you use your attention to witness the dream from the point of view of light. You no longer see everything outside of you as if it's separate from you. You feel the totality of yourself in everything. You feel yourself as the only living being that exists, and you don't just feel it; you *know* it. As we said before, you understand what you are, but not with words. You don't need symbols. If you use symbols to understand what you are, you can get lost in the symbols while trying to understand yourself.

You call yourself a *human*, and perhaps you identify with that symbol, but in China you're not a human; in Spain you're not a human; in Germany you're not a human. *Human* is just one symbol, and what is the meaning of that symbol? You could write an entire book and use thousands of symbols to describe the meaning of *human*, and still you would leave something out, and it's just one symbol! Using symbols to understand what you are is nothing but nonsense. Whatever you *think* you are will never be the truth because symbols are not the truth.

If you say to a cat, "Hey, you dog!" it won't care; it won't answer back. If you say to a person, "Hey, you dog!" that person will surely respond, "I'm not a dog." Some people may be offended, and others may laugh; it will be tragic for some and comic for others, because we're dealing with different points of view. Do animals need to know the symbol for what they are? Well, they don't know, and they don't care. They just are. They don't need symbols to justify their existence.

If someone asks me what I am, I can say, "I am a human being. I am a man. I am made out of energy. I am made out of matter. I am a father, I am a doctor." I can use symbols to identify what I am, to justify what I am, to try to understand myself. But the symbols don't mean anything really. The truth is I don't know what I am. The only thing I know is that I am. I'm alive, and you can touch me. I'm dreaming, and I'm aware that I'm dreaming.

Aside from that, nothing else is important, because everything else is just a story. Symbols will never tell me what I am, or where I came from, and it's not important because I am going back there anyway. That's why one of my biggest heroes is the cartoon character Popeye the Sailor Man, who says, "I am what I am, and that's all that I am." That's wisdom. That's complete acceptance, which means complete respect for what I am, because I am truth. Maybe what I say is not truth, but *I am* truth, and it's the same with you.

You're alive; you do exist, that's true, but what are you? The truth is you don't know. You only know what you believe you are, you know what you learned that you are, you know what you were told that you are, you know what you pretend to be, you know the way you wish to be seen by other people, and for you it may be true. But is it *really* true that you are what you say you are? I don't think so. Whatever you say about yourself is just symbology, and it is completely distorted by your beliefs.

When you finally see yourself without all the knowledge that you've accumulated, the result is: *I am.* I am what I am; you are what you are, and the complete acceptance of whatever you are is what makes the difference. Once you completely accept what you are, you are ready to enjoy life. There's no more judgment, no more guilt, no more shame, no more remorse.

When you leave symbols aside, what remains is the bare truth, pure and simple. You don't need to know what you are, and this is a huge revelation! You don't need to pretend to be what you are not. You can be completely authentic. And because of that, you can deliver a message, and that message is the real you. Your *presence* is the message. It's the same presence you can feel when your first child is born and you finally hold it in your hands. You can feel the presence of the divinity in your hands without understanding anything, without any words.

Every newborn baby has the same presence. It's God, the infinite, an angel incarnate, and we are programmed to react to the presence of a baby. The baby doesn't need to say a word; the presence of the baby says everything. Just its presence awakens the need to give, to protect. When it's your own baby, the instinct is even stronger, and then the presence is really something incredible. That presence awakens your generosity, and you just start giving to your child without expecting anything back, until perhaps a certain point when your child grows up, and it seems as if that presence was lost.

When you were born, your presence was enough to awaken an instinct in the people around you to give you attention, to protect you, to try to fulfill your needs. You still have that presence, but it has been repressed for a long time. It has been waiting to come out. To really feel your presence, you need to be completely aware; you need to see your whole creation from another point of view, from a place where everything is simple. When you're not aware, everything looks completely illogical, and fear takes over and creates the big *mitote*.

The fifth agreement is an important part of recovering what you are, because it uses the power of doubt to break all those spells you've been under. It's a very strong intent for you to use your magic to recover the presence that you lost a long time ago. When all of your attention is not on your story, you can *see* what is real; you can *feel* what is real. When you are not possessed by a symbology, you recover the presence you had when you were born, and the emotions of the people around you respond to your presence. Then you give other people the only thing you really have, which is yourself, your presence, and that makes a huge difference. But this only happens when you become completely authentic.

Just imagine becoming the way you used to be as a very young child, before you understood the meaning of any symbol, before knowledge took over your mind. When you recover your presence, you are just like a flower, just like the wind, just like the ocean, just like the sun, just like the light. You are just like *you*. There is nothing to justify; there is nothing to believe. You are here just to be, for no reason. You have no mission except to enjoy life, to be happy. The only thing you need is just to be the *real* you. Be authentic. Be the presence. Be happiness. Be love. Be joy. Be yourself; that's the main point. That's wisdom.

Those who are not yet wise are searching for perfection; they're searching for God; they're searching for heaven, and trying to find it. Well, there's nothing to search for. It's already here. Everything is within you. You don't have to search for heaven; you are heaven right now. You don't have to search for happiness; you are happiness wherever you are. You don't have to search for the truth; you are the truth. You don't have to search for perfection. That's an illusion. You don't have to search for yourself; you never left yourself. You don't have to search for God; God never left you. God is always with you; you are always with yourself. If you don't see God everywhere, it's because your attention is focused on all those gods you *really* believe in.

The presence of the infinite is everywhere, but if you're in darkness, you don't see what is there. You don't see it because you only see your own knowledge. You guide your creation through that dream, and when your knowledge can't explain what is happening in your life, you feel threatened. What you know is what you want to know, and whatever threatens your knowledge makes you feel insecure. But the moment will come when you realize that knowledge is nothing but a description of a dream.

You are the unknowable. You are here just to be in this moment, in this dream. Being has nothing to do with knowledge. It's not about understanding. You don't need to understand. It's not about learning. You are here to unlearn, and that's it, until one day you realize you know nothing. You only know what you believe, what you learned, just to find out that it wasn't the truth. Socrates, one of the greatest philosophers of all time, took his whole life to get to the point where he said, "As for me, all I know is that I know nothing."

12

BECOMING A SEER

A New Point of View

TWO THOUSAND YEARS AGO, A GREAT MASTER SAID, "And you will know the truth, and the truth will set you free." Well, now you know that the truth is what you are. The next step is to *see* the truth, to see what you are. Only then are you free. Free of what? Free of all the distortions in your knowledge, free of all the emotional drama that is the consequence of believing in lies. When the truth sets you free, the symbols you learned are no longer ruling your world. Then it's not about being right or wrong, or good or bad. It's not about being a winner or a loser. It's not about being young or old, beautiful or ugly. All that is over. It was nothing but symbols.

You'll know that you are totally free when you no longer have to be the you that you pretend to be. This freedom is profound. It's the freedom to be the real you, and it's the greatest gift that you can give yourself.

Imagine living without fear, without judgment, without blame, without guilt, without shame. Imagine living your life without trying to please other people's points of view, and not even your own point of view according to your own book of law. Imagine how different your life would be if you lived with gratitude, love, loyalty, and justice, beginning with yourself. Just imagine the union between you and your body if you were completely loyal to your body, if you were completely grateful for your body, if you treated your body with justice. Imagine being yourself, and not trying to convince anybody of anything. Imagine that just by being yourself, you are happy, and that wherever you go, heaven is going with you, because you *are* heaven. Imagine living with this kind of freedom. Yes, the truth will set you free, but first you need to *see* the truth.

I want you to see if the story of you is the truth or is not the truth. Just witness what *is*, without any judgment, because whatever you're creating is perfect. See your environment, the frame of your dream, all around you. See your beliefs, the way they're reflected in the story of your life. See where your attention is bringing your whole dream. I don't mean for you to *think* about it. I mean for you to *see*, and seeing is not thinking. Is it the truth?

Well, if it's not the truth, now you know that you don't have to believe it. Instead of believing, learn to *see*. What you believe, you distort right away according to your knowledge. But when you let go of knowledge and go beyond symbols, at a certain point in your life, you start to become a seer. A seer is a dreamer who has mastered the dream, who has learned to *see*. Artist, dreamer, messenger, seer — there are so many ways to name you. I prefer to call you an artist because your whole creation is a masterpiece of art.

This is your chance to see your creation, to see what *is*, to see the truth. But first you have to let go of everything that is not truth, everything that is nothing but a superstition or lie. If you're willing to invite the truth, you will find that your story, whatever you say it is, is completely false. You know that the story of you is not the truth. You just need the courage to let go of what you are not, to let go of the past, to detach from your story, because your story is not *you*. The moment you no longer believe all the lies that you have been telling yourself, you find out that it doesn't matter how painful it is; the truth is a million times better than believing in lies.

In any novel, in any movie or real-life drama, the highest point of the story is the moment of truth.

Before then, all of the drama in the story is building and building. The tension keeps escalating until the truth arrives like a tidal wave and destroys all the lies. In the moment of crisis, the lies can't survive the presence of the truth and they disappear. There's no more tension. Peace returns with the truth, and we feel relieved that the drama is over.

Of course, when the truth arrives in your own story, everything you believe feels threatened. Fear takes over and says, "Help! The entire structure of my life, everything I've ever believed in, is falling apart. What am I going to do without all my lies? If I don't believe everything anymore, if I don't gossip anymore, I'll have nothing to say." *Exactly!* This is what I've been trying to tell you.

People ask me, "If I no longer believe all the symbols, if I take my faith out of every word, how can I communicate with anyone? How can I survive in life without the foundation of what I know?" As you can see, the power of doubt is working in their minds, and it's even bigger than before.

Well, if you remember the way you used to be before you learned to speak, when you were just like the rest of the animals, you will see that at that time you could communicate without words. Without using your intellect, without using words, I want you to recover what you used to be long ago, to go back to the authenticity that you had before you learned to speak, and experience the truth. I want you to go directly into your heart, and search for the truth with no words, to find your authentic self, and bring it out with all of your power.

The highest point of your journey back to you is the moment when you finally see yourself through the eyes of truth. If you can see your authentic self, you will love what you see. You see the magnificence of your presence; you see how wonderful and beautiful you are. You see the perfection in you, and this breaks any doubt that anyone else ever put in your head. You see that you are light, that you are *life*, and when you accept your own divinity, you become a better reflection of life.

You are here to enjoy life. You are not here to suffer over your drama or your personal importance. It's not *you*; it doesn't belong to your presence. You are here to be a dreamer, to be an artist, to be a seer. But you cannot be a seer when you only have eyes to see your own story, your own wounds, your own victimization. When you are still focusing on what your mother did to you twenty years ago, or forty years ago, or what your father did, or what your partner did, or what any of the other secondary characters in your story did to you, then you are not seeing the truth. If you are focusing on all that drama, then talking to you is like talking to a wall. Does this ring any bells someplace?

Before you become a seer, you are far from the simplicity of life — very far from it. You believe that you know everything. You have so many great opinions, and you try to impose your opinions on everybody else. Once you become a seer, everything changes. As a seer, you see what people pretend to be, what they express, what they believe they are.

You know that it's not the truth; you know that everybody is just pretending. What are they pretending? You don't know, exactly; you can't read the minds of all those secondary characters that you create. You hardly know what *you're* pretending. But something you can see behind all that pretending is the real person. And how can you not love the real person? Just like you, the real person comes from the infinite. The real person has nothing to do with the symbols that come from the voice of knowledge; the real person has nothing to do with any story.

When you become a seer, you see what is *behind* the story. You understand other people, but they don't understand themselves. There's no way they will understand you, and they don't have to. The majority of humans don't have the awareness that you have. They don't know why they are the way they are. They have no idea; they just survive. They don't have to believe everybody, but they believe everybody anyway. They don't trust themselves at all; they have no idea how great they are. They only see their knowledge, which surrounds them like a wall of fog. Imagine being the only sober person in the middle of a thousand people who are completely drunk. Are you going to have a discussion with people like that? Do you really want to believe them? You know that whatever they say isn't the truth. And you know this because you used to be drunk too, and everything you said wasn't the truth either.

With awareness, you can easily understand how those minds were prepared to become what they are. But just because you have awareness, it doesn't mean that you are better than anyone else. Being aware doesn't make you superior, and it doesn't make you more intelligent. It has nothing to do with intelligence. Knowing this, of course you are completely humble. You just don't care. But there are two ways of "I don't care." There's the way of the victim in the dream of the first attention, and that "I don't care" is just a lie, because victims really do care, and they get very hurt and injured. They have all those emotional wounds that are full of poison and a defense mechanism that says, "Oh, I don't care." Of course they care, and of course you won't believe that "I don't care."

When you're a seer, humans are extremely predictable. You can see that all humans in the dream of the victims are possessed by the main character of their story. This is their point of view — their *only* point of view. The way they see life is very narrow, and it's narrow because their beliefs act like a mirror that only shows them what they believe, and it's obvious that it's not truth at all. They project what they believe on you, and you perceive what they project on you, but you don't take it personally because you don't make the assumption that what they are projecting is true. You know that what they project is what they believe about *themselves*, and you know that because you used to do the same thing.

Once you become a seer, you see everything that other artists do to themselves, but your point of view is completely impersonal. The process of unlearning takes you to a place where there's no longer a judge and a victim in your story. It's just a story, and you know that it's your creation, but it's just as if it's happening to somebody else. You see all the stories; you see all the symbols; you see how people play with all of that, but it has no effect on you. It doesn't offend you, because you are completely immune. You see faces, you love the faces, but you are also aware that there's something that doesn't belong to your dream. It's the personal dream that other artists are dreaming, and you have complete respect for their dream, for their creation.

Respect is a beautiful word, and it's one of the most important symbols that we can understand. Imagine that you had never heard the word before, and let's make it up and agree on a meaning, because just like any other symbol, we need to agree with the symbol or it won't work for us. Respect, like many of the symbols, begins with ourselves, and then it goes out to everyone and everything around us. If we don't respect ourselves, how can we respect anyone or anything else?

When you respect yourself, this means you accept yourself just the way you are. When you respect other people, this means you accept them just the way they are. When you respect everything in nature — the animals, the oceans, the atmosphere, the earth — this means you accept the entire creation just the way it is. When we arrive in this world, everything was created already. It wasn't our choice to see what had to be created or not. It was done, and we respect it. Can we do it better? Maybe, but I don't think so. Then respect is about the complete acceptance of everything that exists just the way it is, not the way we want it to be. This is more or less one meaning of the word *respect*.

Once you accept yourself just the way you are, you no longer have any judgments about yourself. Once you accept everybody else just the way they are, you no longer have any judgments about them. Then something incredible happens in your world: You find peace. You are not in conflict with yourself, and you are not in conflict with anyone else.

All of the conflict that exists in humanity is because there is no respect. Every war is because we didn't respect the other artists' way of life. Instead of respecting their rights, we start imposing what we believe on others. Instead of peace, there is war.

Respect is like a boundary. What we call our *rights* and respect go together. We have our rights, just as everything that exists in the universe has its rights. We live in a world that we share with billions of other beings, and respect makes it possible for all dreamers to live in harmony, to live in peace.

In the dream of the second attention, we begin to create our personal heaven, and when we reach the dream of the third attention, our life *is* heaven. Heaven is a kingdom where we are the king or the queen. I have my personal kingdom and it's heaven, but it wasn't always heaven. It became heaven the moment that I no longer judged myself or anybody else — when I decided to respect my kingdom completely, and when I learned to respect everybody else's kingdom. The fifth agreement is also about respect because I respect other artists when I *listen* to their story. Instead of helping other artists to write their story, I allow them to write their own.

I will never be the one who writes your story, just as I will never allow anyone to write mine. I respect your mind, your dream, your creation. I respect whatever you believe. I respect you when I don't try to tell you how to live your life, how to dress, how to walk, how to talk, how to do whatever you do in your kingdom. As soon as I try to control your kingdom, I'm not respecting you anymore, and we are going to be in a war of control for your kingdom. If I try to control you, in that intent to control you, I lose my freedom. Then my freedom is to let you be whatever you are, whatever you want to be. It's not my job to change your virtual reality. It's my job to change myself.

You are the king or queen of your kingdom. It's your creation; it's where you live, and it's all yours. You are dreaming your kingdom, and you can be intensely happy in your own kingdom. How? First, you need to respect your own kingdom, or very soon that kingdom will be hell and not heaven anymore. Second, you will not allow anyone else to disrespect your kingdom. Whoever disrespects your kingdom is going out of your kingdom. It's your kingdom; it's your life. You have the right to live your own life, in your own way, and there is no wrong way. The wrong way is just another judgment that we create.

Once you have won your personal war, you have no judgments about anything, and other people's judgments don't affect you. Of course you make mistakes like everybody else, but there's perfect justice in your head. You pay only once for every mistake, and because you are kind to yourself, because you love yourself, the payment is very little.

Perhaps these words that I'm sharing with you will have a meaning that makes sense to that voice that lives in your head. And perhaps that voice can start dreaming with this new information, and decide to stop being a tyrant, to stop judging you, to stop punishing you. The day of your last judgment could almost be here. It's up to you. If you can convince the tyrant to stop judging, then very soon everything will change for you.

Imagine that instead of being your adversary, the tyrant becomes your ally, and instead of guiding your life into drama, it helps you to keep the peace. When the tyrant becomes your ally, it never goes against you again; it never sabotages you again. It facilitates whatever you want to create. Then the mind becomes a powerful tool of the spirit; it becomes a powerful ally. The result is a completely different dream: your personal heaven.

In the dream of heaven, you completely surrender to life, knowing that everything is just the way it is. And because you accept everything as it is, you no longer worry about anything. Your life becomes exciting because there's no more fear. You know that you are doing exactly what you are supposed to be doing, and that everything that has happened was meant to happen. Even what you consider your worst mistakes were meant to happen because they have led you to greater awareness. Even the worst thing that can happen to you is meant to happen because it's going to push you to grow.

What is the worst thing that can happen to any of us? To die? We are all going to die, and there's nothing we can do. We can enjoy the ride, or resist it and suffer. Resistance, however, is futile. We are programmed to be what we are, and we can only be whatever we are. But inside our virtual reality, we can go against our own programming, and that's how we create a whole world of resistance. The struggling is just the resistance, and resistance creates suffering.

When you surrender to life, everything changes just like magic. You surrender to that force that is coming through your body, through your mind, and it's a whole new way to see life. It's a way of being. It's being *life*. You are happy because you are *truth*. You are happy wherever you are, whatever you do. Even when you are bored, you enjoy life. Even when you create problems, you enjoy life. You are free, and it's the freedom of a dream master who is not attached to the dream. You hook into the dream with your attention, and you unhook from it whenever you want. The outside dream wants to hook your attention, and you allow it to make the connection, but you can break it at any time. From one moment to another, you can change what you are dreaming and start all over again.

In every moment, you make the choice of what you want to keep, and what you want to let go of. But not with words. You don't need to make a story, but you can if you want to. In your story, you can blame the whole world for whatever is happening to you, or you can take responsibility for your story, be the artist, see the story, and change it in whatever way that you want to change it. You can be rich, or you can be poor. It's not important. You can have fame or not, and it's not important. To have fame in the world of darkness I don't think is fun at all. To be a ruler of hell, I don't think is fun, but it's a choice, and you can make that choice. If you take responsibility for your creation, you can create anything you want in your life. You can rewrite your story; you can re-create your dream. And if you decide to put your love into your creation, you can change all the stories that used to be a drama into the most wonderful, romantic comedies.

Perhaps you're not finished with your story, and who knows if you'll ever finish it or not. Honestly, it's not that important. Whatever you do with your life is not that important. Whatever anybody else does with their life is not important, and it's not your business. Hardly anything is that important. But we can say that one thing is important, and it's *life* itself; it's *intent* by itself, the Creator. The creation is not that important; the manifestation will change day by day, moment to moment, generation to generation. Life is eternal, but your dream only exists while you live in the physical body. Whatever you did here, you won't take with you. You don't need it. You never did; you never will.

But this does not mean that you will not create. Of course, you will create, because it's your nature to create. You are always creating; you are always expressing yourself. You were born an artist, and your art is the expression of your spirit; it's the expression of that force that you are. You know how powerful you are, and that power is real. You know what you learned, and you know that all your knowledge is not real.

The truth is happening right in front of you. To experience life is to experience truth. To *see* the truth makes a huge difference in your world; to *become* the truth is the real goal, because that is the real you. What is not truth is not important. Your desire for the truth, and your love for the truth, is what is important, and that is the real teaching.

13

THE THREE LANGUAGES

What Kind of Messenger Are You?

THE FIFTH AGREEMENT IS THE MOST ADVANCED teaching of the Toltec, because it prepares us to return to what we really are: messengers of truth. We deliver a message every time we speak, and if we don't deliver the truth, it's because we aren't aware of what we really are. Well, the Four Agreements help us to recover awareness of what we are.

They help us to become aware of the power of our word. But the real goal is the fifth agreement, because it takes us beyond symbology and makes us responsible for the creation of every word. The fifth agreement helps us to recover the power of belief that we invested in symbols. And when we go beyond symbols, the power that we find is incredible because it's the power of the artistic creator, the power of life, the *real* us.

The fifth agreement is for what I call *messenger training,* or *angel training,* because it's for messengers who are aware that they have a message to deliver. *Angel* is a Greek word meaning "messenger." Angels really exist, but not the angels of religion with wings. We are all messengers; we are all angels, but we don't have wings, and we don't believe in angels with wings. The religious story about angels with wings is just a symbol, and as a symbol, the wings mean that angels can fly.

Angels fly and they deliver information, a message, and the real message is life, or truth. But there are so many messengers in this world who don't deliver life, who don't deliver truth. The world is populated by billions of messengers, with or without awareness. It's obvious that the majority are without awareness. They are programmed to deliver and receive a message, but they don't know they are messengers. The majority of the humans on earth have no idea that the symbols are their own creation. They have no idea where the power of the symbols comes from, which means that the symbols have complete control over them.

What kind of messengers are they? The answer is obvious. You see the consequences in the world. Just look around, and you will find out what kind of messengers they are. When you find that out, the fifth agreement makes even more sense. *Be skeptical, but learn to listen.* What will make a difference in these messengers? The answer is awareness. That is what messenger training does for us. It helps us to become aware of the kind of message that we are delivering in this world.

From the Toltec point of view, there are only three ways to deliver a message, or we can say that there are only three languages in the world of the humans: the language of gossip, the language of the warrior, and the language of truth.

The language of gossip is the one that all humans speak. Everybody knows how to gossip. When we speak this language, our message is distorted; we gossip about everything around us, but mainly we gossip about ourselves. If we go to another country where people speak a different language, we find that it doesn't matter what symbology they use, they speak like us, in the language of gossip, in what I call the big *mitote*. In the ordinary dream without awareness, the big *mitote* takes over the human mind and creates all the misunderstandings, all the distortions in the way we interpret the meaning of words.

The language of gossip is the language of the victim; it's the language of injustice and punishment. It's the language of hell, because all that gossip is made purely by lies. But humans will always gossip because we are programmed to gossip until something shifts inside of us that is also in the program. This is when we rebel against the gossiping, and the war begins in our head — the war between truth and lies.

The second language is that of the warrior. When we speak this language, sometimes we speak the truth, and sometimes we speak lies, depending on our awareness. Sometimes we believe the lies, which takes us directly to hell, and sometimes we believe the truth, which takes us directly to heaven. But we still *believe*, which means the symbols still have the power of our belief. As warriors, we jump from one dream to the other dream; sometimes we are in heaven, sometimes we are in hell. As you can imagine, the language of the warrior is a thousand times better than the language of gossip, but again, humans are programmed to shift the language we speak, and to speak one more language.

The third language is the language of truth, and when we speak this language, we hardly speak.

At this point, we know without a doubt that the symbols we use are our creation. We know that we give the meaning to all those symbols to communicate with our own kind, and we use symbols with impeccability, the best we can, to deliver our message, to deliver ourselves, because *we* are the message. Finally, there are no more lies, and there are no more lies because we have mastered awareness, because we see ourselves as life, as truth.

The language of truth is very exclusive because it's the language of the dream master, the artist who has mastered the dream. In the world of the master, there is always music, there is always art, there is always beauty. The master artists are always happy. They are at peace, and they enjoy their lives.

These three ways of communicating are what I call the languages of 1-2-3, A-B-C, and Do-Re-Mi. The language of gossip is 1-2-3 because it's simple to learn, and it's the language that everybody speaks. The language of the warrior is A-B-C, because the warrior is the one who rebels against the tyranny of the symbols. The language of truth is Do-Re-Mi, because it's for artists who have music in their heads instead of a big *mitote*.

The language of Do-Re-Mi is the one that I like to speak. My head is always full of music because music distracts the mind, and when the mind is not in the way, it's pure *intent*. I know that all that music in my head is nothing but a dream, but at least I'm not thinking and making a story.

Of course, I can make a story if I want to, and it can be a beautiful story. I can focus my attention on the symbols, and use the symbols that you understand to communicate with you. I can also use the symbols to hear what you say. Usually it is about your own story. You tell me many things that you believe are true, and I know they are not. But when you tell me, I listen, and then I know exactly where you are coming from. I see what perhaps you don't see. I see the *real* you, not what you pretend to be. What you pretend to be is so complicated that I don't even bother to try to understand it. I know it is not *you*. The real you is your presence, and it's as beautiful and wonderful as anything on this earth.

When you see a rose, open and beautiful, its very presence makes you feel wonderful. You don't need to tell yourself how wonderful that rose is; you can see all the beauty and romance of that rose. You smell the rose, and the rose never says a word. You understand the message, but not with words. If you go to a forest, you see birds talking to birds, and trees talking to trees, with another kind of symbology. You can see the inner communication of everything around you, and it's amazing. There are messengers everywhere in this world, but have you ever thought about it?

Have you ever noticed that since you arrived in this world, you've always been delivering a message? Even before you were born, when your mother became aware that she was pregnant, your message was there. Your parents could hardly wait for your arrival, for the moment of your birth. They knew that a miracle was happening, and as soon as you were born, you delivered the message right away with no words. They felt your presence. It was the birth of an angel, and the message was *you*.

You were the message, and you still are the message, but you've been distorted by the reflection of the other messengers. It's not the messengers' fault, it's not your fault, and in fact it's nobody's fault. The distortion is perfect because only perfection exists, but then you grow up, you become aware, and you can choose to deliver a different message. You can choose to become a better reflection of life by changing the language you speak. You can change the way you deliver a message, the way you communicate with yourself and with other people.

Now a simple question for you. I want you to understand the question, but don't allow that voice in your head to answer the question. Just allow these words to go directly into your heart, where you can feel the meaning and intent behind the words. This is the question: *What kind of messenger are you?* This is not a judgment. It's just a little doubt for your mind, but it's a big step into awareness. If you understand the question, then just this little doubt can change your whole life.

What kind of messenger are you? Do you deliver the truth, or do you deliver lies? Do you perceive the truth, or do you only perceive lies? The whole thing is between the truth and lies. This is the core of the problem, and this is what makes all the difference, because all conflict — whether it's inner conflict or conflict between humans — is the result of delivering lies and believing in lies.

What kind of messenger are you? Are you a messenger of gossip and lies? Do you feel comfortable with all the lies, with all the gossip, with all the drama that comes as a result of believing in lies? Is that what you share with everyone around you? Is that what you teach your children? Do you still blame your parents for your troubles? Remember, they did the best they could. If your parents abused you, it wasn't personal. It was due to their own fears; it was due to what they believed. If they abused you, it's because they were also abused. If they hurt you, it's because they were also hurt. It's an ongoing chain of action-reaction. Are you going to continue being a part of that chain, or is it over with you?

What kind of messenger are you? Are you the warrior who struggles in between heaven and hell? Do you still believe people who tell you, "This is the truth"? Do you still believe your own lies? What kind of message are you delivering to the people you love the most if the message that you deliver to yourself is guiding you into hell? What kind of message are you delivering to your children, whom you love so much? What kind of message are you delivering to your beloved, to your parents, to your siblings, to your friends, to everyone around you?

What kind of messenger are you? If you tell me what kind of dream you're creating for yourself, I will tell you what kind of messenger you are. How do you treat yourself? Are you kind to yourself? Do you respect yourself? Do you respect other people? How do you feel about yourself? Do you even like yourself? Are you proud of yourself? Are you happy with yourself? Is there any drama or injustice in your dream? Does your dream have a judge and a victim? Is it a dream of predators, a dream of violence? If so, your dream is distorting your message. The judge, the victim, and all those voices in your head are distorting everything.

Right now, you're delivering a message to yourself and to everyone else around you. You're always delivering a message, and you're always receiving a message from one mind to another mind. What is the message that you are delivering in this world? Is the message impeccable? Do you even notice that you are always using symbols?

Just observe the messages that you're delivering. Are the words that you're speaking coming from the truth, or are they coming from the voice of knowledge, the tyrant, the big judge? Who's delivering the message? Is it the *real* you? This is your dream. If it's not the real you, then who is delivering the message? Isn't that a good question?

Can you see the impact of the words that you reflect to others as you speak? Just imagine that you are talking to a wall. Don't expect an answer. It's not for the wall to hear what you're saying. It's for you to see what is coming out of your mouth. It's for you to begin to see the impact of your words on everything around you. By talking to a wall, your message becomes more and more clear. After that, the importance of impeccability becomes obvious.

Now I want you to use your imagination to see the kind of interactions that you have had in your entire life with other people. I'm sure you have lots of memories of your interactions with everybody around you. People are always delivering messages to you, and you're always perceiving their messages. What kind of messengers are the other people in your life? What kind of messages did they deliver to you during your whole life? How did all those messages affect you? Out of all the messages that you received from other people, how many of those messages did you agree with and take as your own?

How many of those messages are you still delivering now? If you're delivering somebody else's messages, whose messages are you delivering?

Just have the awareness of the kind of messages that you've delivered your entire life, and the kind of messages that you've received your entire life. You don't need to judge anyone, including yourself. Just ask: *What kind of messenger am I? What kind of messengers are the other people in my life?* This is a big step in the mastery of awareness; it's a big step in being a seer.

Once you are aware of the messages that you're delivering, and the messages that other people are delivering to you, your point of view shifts strongly and firmly. You clearly see the messages that other people are delivering to you, and you clearly see what kind of messenger they are. Then the moment comes when your awareness is so expansive that you clearly see the messages that you're delivering to other people. You see exactly what kind of messenger you are. You see the effect of your words, the effect of your actions, the effect of your presence.

You are always delivering a message to everyone and everything around you, but mainly you are always delivering a message to yourself. *What is the message?* That message is the most important one, because that message affects your whole life. Are you the master who delivers the truth? Are you the victim who delivers lies? Well, it doesn't really matter if you are the master, or if you are the messenger of gossip, full of poison, or if you are the warrior and you go up and down, from heaven to hell, from hell to heaven. You deliver the information that you have inside you. It's not right or wrong, or good or bad; it's what you know. It's what you learned your whole life, and it doesn't really matter what you learned. It doesn't really matter what you have been teaching, what you have been sharing.

What really matters is to be what you really are — to be authentic, to enjoy life, to be love. And not the *symbol* of love that humans have distorted, but *real* love — the feeling you can't put into words, the love that is the result of being what you really are.

Always remember: You are the force that's creating everything in existence. You are the force that opens a flower and moves the clouds, and the earth, and the stars, and the galaxies. Whatever your message, love yourself anyway, *because* of what you are, because you *respect* what you are. You don't have to be different unless you decide that you love yourself so much that you are no longer satisfied with the kind of messenger you are.

Perhaps you've misused the word because you were innocent, because you didn't have awareness. But what happens when you have awareness and you're still doing it? Once you have awareness, you cannot claim innocence anymore. You know exactly what you're doing, and whatever you're doing is still perfect, but now it's your decision; it's your choice. Now the question becomes: What kind of message do you *choose* to deliver? Is it truth or is it lies? Is it love or is it fear? My choice is to deliver a message of truth and love. What is yours?

Epilogue

Help Me to Change the World

IF YOU ARE NO LONGER SATISFIED WITH THE KIND of messenger you are, if you want to become a messenger of truth and love, then I invite you to participate in a new dream for humanity, one in which *all* of us can live in harmony, truth, and love.

In this dream, people of all religions and all philosophies are not just welcome, but respected. Each of us has the right to believe whatever we want to believe, to follow any religion or philosophy we want to follow. It doesn't matter whether we believe in Christ, Moses, Allah, Brahma, Buddha, or any other being or master; everybody is welcome to share this dream. I don't expect you to believe all my stories, but if they resonate inside you, if you can feel the truth *behind* the words, then let's make one more agreement: *Help me to change the world.*

Of course, the very first question is: How are you going to change the world? The answer is easy. By changing *your* world. When I ask you to help me to change the world, I'm not talking about planet Earth. I'm referring to the virtual world that exists in your head. The change begins with you. You will not help me to change the world if you don't change your own world first.

You will change the world by loving yourself, by enjoying life, by making your personal world a dream of heaven. And I ask you for your help because you are the only one who can change your world. If you decide that you want to change your world, the easiest way is by using the tools that are nothing but common sense. The Five Agreements are tools to change your world. If you are *impeccable with your word*, if you *don't take anything personally*, if you *don't make assumptions*, if you *always do your best*, and if you are *skeptical while listening*, there won't be any more war in your head; there will be peace.

If you practice the Five Agreements, your world becomes better, and you want to share your happiness with the people you love. But changing the world is not about changing the secondary characters of your story. If you want to change the world, *your* world, the way to do it is by changing the main character of your story. If you change the main character, then just like magic, all the secondary characters will start to change also. When you change, your children will change, because the message that you deliver to them will change. The message that you deliver to your wife or your husband will change. Your relationship with your friends will change. Perhaps more important, your relationship with yourself will change.

When you change the message you deliver to yourself, you are happier, and just by being happier, the people who live around you will also benefit. Your effort is really for everyone, because your joy, your happiness, your heaven are contagious. When you're happy, the people around you are happy too, and it inspires them to change their own world.

We represent a whole legacy, and when I say *we*, I'm speaking for all humans. Our legacy is love; it's joy; it's happiness. Let's enjoy this world. Let's enjoy one another. We are meant to love one another, not to hate one another. Let's stop believing that our differences make us superior or inferior to one another. Let's not believe that lie. Let's not be afraid that our different colors make us different people. Who cares? It's just another lie. We don't have to believe all the lies and superstitions that have control of our lives. This is the time to end all the lies and superstitions that are not helping anybody. This is the time to end the fanaticism. We can return to the truth, and be messengers of truth.

We have a message to deliver, and that message is our legacy. When we were children, we received the legacy of our parents and our ancestors. We received a wonderful world, and it's our turn to offer our children and grandchildren a planet where they can live as wonderfully and as well as we do now. We can stop destroying our planet; we can stop destroying one another. The humans can live in harmony. It's incredible what we can do if we really want to do it. All we need is to be aware of what we are doing, and to return to our authenticity.

I know that we have our differences because we live in our personal dream, but we can respect one another's dream. We can agree to work together, knowing that each of us is the center of our own dream. Each one of us has our own beliefs, our own story, our own point of view. There are billions of different points of view, but it's the same light, the same force of life behind each one of us.

Help me to change the world is an invitation to be authentic, to be free. Open your heart to receive this agreement. I'm not asking you to *try* to change the world. Don't *try* to do it. Just do it. Take the action today. The legacy that we leave to our children and grandchildren can be magnificent. We can change our whole way of thinking, and show them how to have a love affair with life. We can live in our personal heaven that follows us wherever we go. It's not true that we come to this planet to suffer. This beautiful planet Earth is not a valley of tears. Our new way of thinking can replace all those lies and take us to a wonderful place to live life.

Wherever I go, I hear people say that we come here with a mission, that we have something to do in this life, something to transcend. Whatever it is, I don't know. I believe that we come here with a mission, but our mission is not really to transcend anything. The mission that you have, and the same mission is true for all of us, is to make yourself happy. The "how" could be millions of different ways of doing what you love to do, but the mission of your life is to enjoy every single moment of your life.

We know that sooner or later our physical bodies will no longer exist. We only have a few sunrises, a few sunsets, a few full moons that we can enjoy. This is our time to be alive, to be fully present, to enjoy ourselves, to enjoy one another.

In the last century, science and technology have grown so fast, but psychology has stayed far behind. It's time for psychology to catch up with science and technology. It's time for us to change our beliefs about the human mind, and what I see right now is almost an emergency, because with computers and the Internet the way they are right now, lies can go all around the world very quickly and get completely out of control.

The time is coming when humans will no longer believe in lies. We begin with ourselves, but the goal is to change the entire humanity, not just our own world. But how can we change the entire humanity if we don't change our own world first? Of course, it's not easy to separate, because in reality we have to do both at the same time.

Then let's make a difference in this world. Let's win the war in our head, and change the world. How long will it take for the entire world to change? Two, or three, or four generations? The truth is that we don't care how long it will take. We are not in a hurry, but we have no time to lose. Help me to change the world.

DON MIGUEL RUIZ

Don Miguel Ruiz is the international bestselling author of *The Four Agreements* (a *New York Times* bestseller for over seven years), *The Mastery of Love*, and *The Voice of Knowledge*. His books have sold nearly eight million copies in the United States, and have been translated into dozens of languages worldwide. For over three decades, don Miguel has shared his unique blend of ancient wisdom and modern-day awareness through lectures, workshops, and journeys to sacred sites around the world.

DON JOSE RUIZ

Don Jose Ruiz grew up in a world where anything was possible. From the moment he could speak, he became an apprentice of his *nagual* (shaman) father, don Miguel Ruiz, and his *curandera* (healer) grandmother, Mother Sarita. As a teenager, he traveled to India to study with friends of his father, and at the age of twenty-three, he became the successor to the family lineage. In the tradition of his ancestors, don Jose has dedicated his life to sharing the teachings of the ancient Toltec. For the past ten years, he has been lecturing and leading classes across the United States, and at sacred sites around the world.

For information about current programs offered by don Miguel Ruiz, don Jose Ruiz, and don Miguel Ruiz, Jr., please visit:

www.miguelruiz.com

JANET MILLS

Janet Mills is the founder and publisher of Amber-Allen Publishing. She is the editor and coauthor of the Toltec Wisdom Series by don Miguel Ruiz, and the editor of Deepak Chopra's international best-selling title *The Seven Spiritual Laws of Success.* Her life's mission is to publish books of enduring beauty, integrity, and wisdom, and to inspire others to fulfill their most cherished dreams.

Also by don Miguel Ruiz

The Four Agreements *

Based on ancient Toltec wisdom, The Four Agreements offer a powerful code of conduct that can rapidly transform our lives to a new experience of freedom, true happiness, and love. Available in cloth, paperback, illustrated edition, e-book, and audiobook.

The Four Agreements Companion Book *

Additional insights, practice ideas, questions and answers about applying The Four Agreements, and true stories from people who have already transformed their lives. Available in paperback and e-book.

The Mastery of Love *

Ruiz shows us how to heal our emotional wounds, recover the joy and freedom that are our birthright, and restore the spirit of playfulness that is vital to loving relationships. Available in cloth, paperback, e-book, and audiobook.

The Four Agreements Toltec Wisdom Collection

This three-book boxed set offers don Miguel Ruiz's most widely acclaimed works, including The Four Agreements, The Mastery of Love, and The Voice of Knowledge. All three books in the collection are paperback.

ALSO BY DON MIGUEL RUIZ

The Circle of Fire (Formerly published as *"Prayers"*)
A beautiful collection of essays, prayers, and guided meditations that will inspire and transform your life. Available in paperback, e-book, and Spanish (*"Oraciones"*).

The Voice of Knowledge *
In this breakthrough book, Ruiz reminds us of a profound and simple truth: The only way to end our emotional suffering and restore our joy in living is to stop believing in lies — mainly about ourselves. Available in paperback and e-book.

Toltec Wisdom Card Decks
Each beautifully illustrated card deck contains 48 pearls of wisdom from Ruiz's bestselling books: *The Four Agreements*, *The Mastery of Love*, *The Voice of Knowledge*, and *The Fifth Agreement*.

* *Also Available in Spanish*

ed

For information about other bestselling titles from
Amber-Allen Publishing, please visit us online at
www.amberallen.com
or call (800) 624-8855